More praise for *Stepchildren S*

"As 'Mom' in a blended family of yours, mine and ours, I could have a used the insights and perspectives of the children interviewed in Susan's book—and I wonder what my own now-grown children would say if I asked some of the same thoughtful questions."
Jennifer Read
Stepmom
Austin, Texas

"I counsel those whose stepfamily experiences have left them feeling alone, guilty and fearful. *Stepchildren Speak* is the first book to give stepchildren of all ages the ability to see their experiences represented in the stories of others. Thank you for this invaluable resource."
Fran Chalin
Clergy of Congregation Beth Chayim Chadashim
Los Angeles, CA

"As a divorce lawyer who works everyday with families struggling with divorce and remarriage, I plan to give this book to all my clients. The stepchildren's insights and advice will help them adjust to their new families and will help me as I counsel my clients."
Steve Larin
Family Lawyer
Los Angeles, CA

"*Stepchildren Speak* has many implications for teachers. It opens a window into the inner lives of children growing up in stepfamilies. No wonder so many students look to their teachers to be dependable and there for them in ways that have nothing to do with academics."
Leigh Ann Orr
Teacher
Los Angeles, CA

■■■■■■■■■■■■■■■■■■■■■■■■■■■■■■■

Stepchildren Speak:

10 Grown-up Stepchildren Teach Us How to Build Healthy Stepfamilies

by

Susan Philips

AYWN Publications

Write to AYWN Publications, 1209 Officers' Row, Vancouver, WA 98661, or call 360-695-1010 for more information.

Visit our web site at www.aywnpublications.com

ISBN 1-893471-09-8

Library of Congress Control Number: 2004110186

1. Stepfamilies   2. Parents

3. Family   4. Divorce

Published in the United States by AYWN Publications, 1209 Officers' Row, Vancouver, WA 98661

Cover design by Stephanie Kleinman and Dyanne Cano, Los Angeles, CA

Author photo by Jacob Pinger

I dedicate this book
to my son Jake and stepchildren David, Susan,
and Maxie for teaching me how to become
a better person and a better parent,
and to my own parents Mary and Connie
for "rolling with the punches."

Acknowledgments

As a first-time published author, I have many people to thank.

To the stepchildren: I want to thank the ten stepchildren in this book, along with the dozens of others I interviewed in preparation, for their commitment to helping stepfamilies. It was not easy for them to tell and retell their stories. Thankfully, they stayed the course, never once uttering those feared words—"Not another question." They were honest, direct, and frequently funny; and while their stories are full of sentiment, they are never sentimental. Needless to say, this book could not have been written without them.

To my editor and publisher Frances Caldwell: Thank you for taking a chance with a first-time writer. When others turned me down, you took me under your skillful and patient wings. I can never thank you enough.

To Ruth: Thank you for your support and gentle guidance as we moved professionally and personally through the process of giving birth to this book.

To my large extended family: A big thanks to all of you for always putting the interests of the children above all others.

To my husband Art: Thanks for your unwavering support and encouragement over these past years. You never doubted me even as I doubted myself.

To all the grandparents: To Mary and Connie, Russ and Peg, and Rose and Ed for always "being there" for my son and stepchildren, rain or shine, good times and bad. You never wavered. I hope I can fill your shoes with my own grandchildren: Mayan Isabelle, Griffin Estes, Mina Tikal, and others to come (hint hint).

To everyone who contributed: To all the people who gave me feedback on the book at different stages, my son Jake for taking my photo, and my stepdaughter Susan for suggesting I ask the stepchildren about their concept of family. "I think you'll find their answers quite interesting," she said. She was right.

Table of Contents

■■■■■■■■■■■■■■■■■■■■■■■■■■■■■■■■■■

Foreword

Ruth Tavlin
Marriage and Family Therapist
Los Angeles, CA
April 2004

This is not just another book on stepfamilies and what you should do or not do. It is much more. This book is different from the others on the market in that it offers a rare opportunity to learn about the experience of growing up in stepfamilies from the children themselves. Most of the other books on divorce and remarriage are told from the perspective of the parents and stepparents. In this book, we allow the children to guide us through the challenges of living through divorce and remarriage.

I have been a marriage and family therapist for over thirty years, and during that time, I have had a special interest in working with parents, stepparents, and stepchildren as they work out new family relationships. I have listened carefully to their concerns and questions. From parents I hear, "My 'ex' and I don't agree about what is best, but we both want to parent our child. What should I do?" The stepparent's lament, "How do I relate to this angry, sullen child? What is my role?" Teenagers ask, "How is this going to change my life? Who do I have to listen to?"

For me, the stories in this book validate the experience of many parents, stepparents, and teenagers as they struggle with these new and complex relationships. Parents can see how important it is for them to work together as they create two families. Stepparents will get new insight into what they can ask of their new partner to help build easier relationships with their stepchildren. Teenagers will get some helpful tips on how to juggle different family relationships and get the support they need from other adults.

Not only does the book validate the experience, it is also valuable because it demonstrates what therapists hope will happen—that clients will heal. For these stepchildren, healing occurred in the process of telling their stories. As you will see, many arrived at a deeper understanding and acceptance of their parents and themselves. Others came to the realization that even with the best of intentions, we sometimes hurt the people we love. For all of them, it provided a deeper look at their experiences.

As you read their stories, you will see that the stepchildren have grown into sensitive, independent, competent, resilient adults. They are serious and cautious about their relationships. Do they experience bouts of depression, loneliness, and insecurity? Yes. Do you know anyone who lives in our world who doesn't? Did these children have an extra challenge living in more than one kind of family? Yes. Are all their problems the result of their parents' divorce and remarriage? Yes and no. As the medical director of the family counseling agency where I work reminds us when we try to determine the "cause" of a child's problem, "It's always about everything." These children help us understand what the "everything" is all about. As they do, you will laugh and cry. Hopefully you will see yourself in these stories. You will learn. I did.

This book has also been important for personal reasons. I too went through a divorce. My two sons, now thirty-two and twenty-eight, grew up in two households in two different cities, in Los Angeles with me, and in Oakland with their father, stepmother, and stepbrother. Needless to say, we spent a lot of time in airports. Working on this book with Susan over the past few years has given my sons and me a chance to discuss their growing-up experiences with a new candor. I began to talk with them about some of the difficult times we experienced but couldn't talk about as we were living through them. We have been able to hear each other now without feeling defensive or fearful that someone will be angry or hurt. Like the stepchildren, my sons and I have gone through a healing process.

Stepchildren Speak adds an important dimension to the work that has already been done in the field. Susan has added the missing piece of the children's experiences. She took the stepchildren on a journey back, she asked probing questions, listened to the answers, knew the next question to ask, and understood the importance of the process. With Susan's guidance and the openness of the stepchildren, we have an opportunity to learn how to create healthier family relationships in the fullest sense of the word. More importantly, it gives us hope as we continue to struggle with the challenge of creating one, two, many families, each one providing the necessary love, safety, and sense of belonging.

■■■■■■■■■■■■■■■■■■■■■■■■■■■■■■■

Introduction

When my husband Art proposed marriage in front of the fruit section of our local supermarket on our regular Saturday night "hot date" (where else do you go when you have four kids at home?), neither of us had the foggiest notion of what was in store. All we knew was that we were in love, and we believed that everything else would magically work itself out. After all, we were from the 60's. Then reality struck, and my entire life changed forever. My family, which for twelve years had been my son Jake and I, expanded exponentially to include my new husband and his three children David, Susan (aka "Little Susan"), and Maxie, not to mention all the supporting characters that accompany any new stepfamily— my ex-husband and his new wife, my husband's former partner and the mother of my three stepchildren, several sets of grandparents, aunts, uncles, cousins, and lots of past and current friends. Things became rather complicated, interesting but complicated.

And it seemed *everyone* had an opinion. I can still see the incredulous look on my mother's face when I told her I was marrying Art. "What are you, nuts? Why can't you just date the guy?" She had her point. Dating is one thing; living together and marriage are quite another, and it became clear rather quickly that despite all my good intentions, I had no idea how much skill it would take to deal with the almost daily onslaught of challenges and questions that confronted us. What should my role be? Should I be a friend? A parent? Should I discipline the children or leave that to their father and mother? What happens when my husband and I disagree (which happened often, especially around that tricky issue of money)? And despite the fact that we were from the 60's, I was not a hippie mom. My husband's kids called him Art; my son called me Mom, not Susan. "Sounds like you're more like a friend than a dad," I would say. And there were lots of questions around the division of household chores. Who should do the dishes, feed the dog, do the laundry, and cook the meals (or, in our case, pick up the take-out)? And what happens when the kids don't do their chores? There were so many things to work out, and so many things that could and did cause problems. And the stakes were high. Our four kids had already experienced too many losses in their short lives; one more was not an option.

Like practically everyone else in my generation, I had no experience with this. When my three brothers and I were growing up, divorce was so rare, so shocking, that I can remember as if it were yesterday how sorry I felt for the children on our block whose parents were divorced. I can remember the hushed voices when the kids were around. "He is from a broken family," they would whisper. A broken family. That can't be good. How could these kids ever be happy, ever feel whole? And yet flash one generation later and it is rare to find children who aren't from "broken families," who don't live in stepfamilies.

The statistics are telling. The first we are familiar with—half of all marriages end in divorce. What people may not know is that 75 percent of the 1.2 million people who divorce each year remarry, and most bring children into their new families. Most of these second marriages, a staggering 60 percent, also end in divorce, and if this trend continues, and there is no reason to think it won't, by the year 2011, more children will be living in stepfamilies than in "intact" families.

Fortunately, there is help out there. When I became

a stepmom twenty years ago, there were almost no resources to help stepfamilies. Today they are on the cultural radar screen, with web sites, chat rooms, support
groups, books, magazines, radio and television talk shows,
and even movies and situation comedies to help us adjust
to living in stepfamilies. For the most part, the discussion
about stepfamilies centers on the role of the stepparents,
especially stepmothers. Through their experiences, we
learn how to deal with the inevitable anger, resentment,
and fear that many stepchildren feel when their parents
divorce and remarry. We also learn how to build trust,
forge bonds, and establish an appropriate level of authority with stepchildren.

This, as my mom was fond of saying, "is all well and
good," yet as I reviewed the movies and television shows,
and read through the dozens of new books and magazines,
I was left with a nagging feeling that while they offered
important advice, I was nonetheless hearing only one side
of the story, seeing only one piece of the picture. And I
wondered—what if I were to ask stepchildren themselves
to tell me how they would go about building trust and
forging bonds with stepchildren? What if I were to ask
them what they thought was the appropriate level of authority for a stepparent or how they would deal with an
angry and scared stepchild? What would they say? And
that, as we say in teaching, was my "aha moment." That
was when I understood what my contribution to the lit-
erature on stepfamilies might be: I would provide an opportunity for stepchildren to tell us adults how to build
stepfamilies that work.

Trained as a journalist as well as a teacher, I forged
ahead. Given the high divorce rate, finding stepchildren to
interview was the easy part. They are everywhere, from
all parts of the country, social classes, and ethnic groups.
And every one I asked (and I asked dozens) wanted to tell

their story, and each had two or three friends waiting in the wings to tell their stories. The hard part was deciding which from the dozens I initially interviewed, I would include in the book. For help on this and other matters, I turned to my good friend and colleague Ruth Tavlin, who has been a marriage and family therapist for over thirty years. Ruth, who also wrote the foreword to the book, became my "consultant." With her gentle guidance, I selected my stepchildren, refined my questions, and set out on a journey that would take me deep into the lives of ten stepchildren, a journey that would move me to tears, cause me to reflect on my own experiences as a stepmother, and ultimately show me the extraordinary resiliency of children.

In this book you will meet these ten stepchildren. They are in their late twenties and early thirties, able to look back on their experiences growing up in stepfamilies with some perspective. Six are females and four are males. Seven are Anglo, two Hispanic, and one African American. They come from Puerto Rico, Minnesota, Colorado, and California. Seven were under five when their parents divorced, and three were adolescents. As you will see, each has a different story to tell; yet together they paint a vivid picture of how it feels to be a stepchild. As you read their stories, you will learn about the challenges of moving back and forth between families, constantly struggling to fit into different households with different personalities, routines, and, at times, even different value systems. You will learn about how these experiences have shaped their lives and their view of marriage and family, and you will learn from their stories what we as parents and stepparents can do and say to create healthy and loving new families.

By allowing us to enter into their lives, to feel their hurt, laugh at their funny stories, and rejoice in their triumphs, the stepchildren help us understand, truly understand. This emotional understanding, more than any list of dos and don'ts, will help all of us become better parents and stepparents to our children. I am certain that I would have been a better stepmom to my three stepchildren, and a better mother to my own son had I had this understanding twenty years ago when I said "yes" to my husband in front of the fruit section of our local supermarket.

■■■■■■■■■■■■■■■■■■■■■■■■■■■■■■■■■

Sophia

Sophia is thirty-one years old and lives alone. Her parents divorced when she was nine and each remarried within a year. Her mother divorced again when Sophia was sixteen and recently remarried. She has five siblings: two brothers, a half-brother from her mother's second marriage, and a half-brother and sister from her father's second marriage. Sophia is studying for her Ph.D. in Public Health.

Sophia's Story

My parents divorced when I was nine, and each re-married within six to eight months. So I became a step-child within a year of my parents' divorce and instantly had two stepbrothers because my stepfather had two sons from a previous marriage. I don't remember feeling bad about new siblings. I do remember feeling bad about the divorce and blaming my mother. I never blamed my father. He was the saint in the relationship in my view. But what ended up happening is that I bonded with my stepfather very quickly, in part because my father stopped being a major part of our lives. He left a vacuum, and my stepfather filled it. At first I resented my stepfather, but I got over it and came to love him very much.

It was different with my stepmom. My father moved away and I saw my stepmom only once a year, so there wasn't that day-to-day interaction. I remember thinking she was very good for my father, but I have never loved her as a parent. I see her as my father's companion.

A Matter of Geography

My life as a stepchild went through multiple geographic spaces. My parents divorced in Puerto Rico. My father moved to San Juan, the capitol. Even though it wasn't very far, it took about two and a half hours to get there, so distance became a barrier to seeing him. When my parents were both on the island, we saw my father about every two weeks. Then in 1985 my mom, stepfather, and brothers migrated to Los Angeles. After that we saw my father about once a year. Geography played a really important role in how often we saw my father and how close we feel to him today.

To this day I will tell you that I consider home wherever my mom is, which is in two primary places—Puerto Rico and Los Angeles. It's Los Angeles (even though my mother is no longer there) because of a tight community of people I love. It's my extended family. Home is not where my father is. Home is a space where you feel comfortable, where you let go of the many layers of persona you put out to the world. I don't think I've ever felt that comfortable with my dad.

Stepmother

The relationship with my stepmother has been, over all, a positive and respectful one. She never tried to be a parental figure, and I never saw her as a threat to my mother's status. I never felt that she tried to replace my mother in any way; she is my father's wife. I am not exactly sure why this happened, but I think that the fact that she was never a key player in my day-to-day life is critical. As I got older, I saw even less of my dad and consequently even less of her.

When we were together, she played the role of a buddy, offering advice in aspects of my life that my mother tended to ignore or not care about (make-up, dress, etc.). She is different from my mom and has other priorities in life—the creation of a warm, safe home is a belief shared by both, but how they conduct themselves is different. When we visited her and my dad, she made it a special time. I feel that she has been a positive influence on my dad. She reminded him to call us or send notes. I believe that she is responsible for much of the contact that we did have with my father. It was her handwriting on the birthday and Christmas cards, not my dad's.

In my late twenties, I moved to Washington, D.C. to go to school and also to get closer to my father and his family. I felt unconditional support from her. She allowed me to move into her home, and she didn't have to do that. I recognize that had she wanted to be a barrier, she easily could have been. She's not a parental figure but a nice aunt or a good friend. When my father did put limits on time spent in their home, it came from him. I never felt reproach or ambivalence from her.

Stepfather

My stepfather was in my life from the time I was nine to sixteen. He had two sons from a previous marriage, but I was the only girl so I had a special status. I was basically his daughter. I do not remember feeling anger towards him, but my grandmother has talked about much anger and, yes, fury I felt toward him and my mother for my parents' divorce. More than anything, now as an adult looking back, I remember him with so much fondness. He was my father in so many ways. I grew a great deal with him— as a child turning into a woman, as an artist, as a human being that valued tenderness and imagination. He was passionate and compassionate and gave me an alternative to what I sensed was the father figure.

He was everything that my father was not—fun, loving, creative, and spontaneous. Unfortunately, he was also an alcoholic. But in my adolescence, those negatives were better than the alternatives. Now that I have developed a relationship with my father, I know that he is quite different from my stepfather; one is not better than the other. But as a teenager, I placed my stepfather on a pedestal. I compensated for my father's absence by turning my stepfather into a god. And when my mom and stepfather divorced, I once again blamed my mom. It is easy to blame the constant love in your life; there is no risk or fear of loss. I feared losing the "fathers" of my life; I could never blame them because that would make them human.

He's not in our lives since the divorce because of alcoholism issues and what not. It was a horrible loss. It was more difficult than the loss of my own father. There was a point in our life where I loved him more than my own father. He played a more immediate role in my day-to-day life. He was there to wake me for school, to check in with me to see how I was feeling, to find out who I was. He was there. He was my daddy. We were a codependent family around the alcoholic. He opted out of our lives perhaps because it was easier. He left and we haven't seen him since.

Father

With my dad, it's been a roller coaster ride. As a child I remember him being very loving and present in our lives. He was the playful one and my mother was the disciplinarian. It was my mom who got us ready for school; it was my mom who got up in the middle of the night when we were crying. My dad was good to be with if you wanted to go to the park and play basketball. It was my mom who was the constant.

What I feel more than anything is an incredible sense of loss. He lost out on our childhood. He was not there. Maybe we talked once a month while I was growing up and there were always gifts, but he just wasn't there for the struggles and the joys and the sadness of what it meant to be a child. It was my mother who was there. He sent that monthly check but that wasn't enough.

In 1998, I made a conscious effort to get to know him. I remember calling up and telling him that I was moving to D.C., that I was doing it because I wanted to get to know him. I told him that I didn't know him and he didn't know me, and that more than anything I wanted to get to know his children. I knew based on my own recollection of my childhood that it was now or never in terms of getting to know my half-brother and -sister. They welcomed me, all of them, with open arms. I lived with them for four months and it was beautiful. And it was the first time that I had gotten to know my father as an adult.

As a result of the time spent with my father, I reached the point where I could tell my mom, "I'm sorry. I don't blame you anymore." I finally got to know what my father was really like. I love him to death, but he isn't the beautiful god figure that I had imagined him to be all these years. I got to see him as a man. I'm really glad that I was able to reach out and be the adult in the relationship, because I don't think he has the skills to do that. What's been the challenge is that my two brothers do not have a relationship with my father and don't necessarily want one. I need to respect that and not push my agenda on them.

The first and only big drama occurred after I found my own place. At first I spent every weekend with him and his family. And then I had this really difficult conversation with my dad where he put boundaries to the time I could spend with the family. What I heard was that I was being disruptive to his family. It was such a painful conversation. I think my dad thought he was losing control of his son and daughter in this second family. When I was there, I brought to the table a different set of norms and way of living. I am my mother's child. I don't doubt that that is true. I would come with stories of adventures. My lifestyle is very different from my father's. I told him that he needed to understand that he hadn't been a part of our lives and that he didn't know me. He didn't know any of us. What ended up happening is that I continued visiting them, but less and less. I found more balance.

I won't ever be as close to my father as I am to my mother, but the most amazing thing is how close I am to my dad's two kids. I don't go to my dad now for any of the parental things like money or advice, especially not money. It's an adult-to-adult relationship.

Mother

My mom has been the sun for all of us. She has been the life support, the financial support, and the disciplinarian. She's been everything. She is, was, and continues to be the force around which we all revolve. Even as I was growing up, the love was there. I blamed her for the divorce. We never talked about it. It wasn't until after I lived with my dad four years ago that we talked about it.

My brothers and I didn't want her to marry for the third time until our youngest brother was out of the house. We didn't want him to go through the stepparent dynamic. We reached a compromise with her. She agreed not to marry until our youngest brother was out of the house, but they would live together. I don't think this was an issue for our brother, but the three oldest ones who had gone through the stepparent thing said, "No, don't do it." Not because it was negative, but because we feared that it would be difficult to negotiate.

Siblings

Describing my siblings is such a complicated task. When my mom and my stepdad met, he was raising two sons by himself. When we first all got married, all of a sudden it was my oldest brother, Jose, my younger brother Raul, my stepdad's two sons, and I. Later my mom and stepdad had Charlie together. My dad and stepmom have two children, Nancy and Jordan.

My brother Jose and I are the closest in age, and we have the typical relationship. We fought. I always felt protective towards him but I also teased him. We are equals.

My brother Raul is five years younger than me. He was the baby for a really long time, and so my relationship with him is older sister and baby brother. But he is a very independent man. He spent the least time with our father. Out of all of us, he knows the least about our dad. He lost the most and he didn't necessarily gain the most because he was a boy. He and our new stepdad have a good relationship.

My half-brother Charlie is the son of my mom and stepdad. He suffered a big loss at five at my mom's second divorce. He is 100 percent mom, even following my mom's career path. My brothers played a father figure to him. My mom's father has also played a father role.

Jordan and Nancy are the son and daughter of my dad and stepmom. I was not raised with them but when I sought out my father in 1998, I began the process of getting to know them. Part of my motivation for getting to know my father was that I wanted to know these children before they grew up completely. Nancy is now fifteen and Jordan is eighteen. They are great kids.

Grandparents

What I consider my nuclear family consists of my mom, my three brothers, and my maternal grandparents.

My grandfather (Abuelo Arturo*)* died last November and my family is still very much adjusting to his death. I think of him now and really just want to cry because I miss him terribly. He was a wonderful man who became our father when our biological one did not step up to this role. He was like this superman who played the grandfather role by spoiling us—a 24-hour ATM who gave us money when my mom had none to give, a father who was our caretaker and our companion at all the father-children events. He died at ninety-six or ninety-eight years of age, depending on when he was born, which fluctuated depending on how my grandfather was feeling at any particular moment.

I have this very clear image of him picking us up after school. I must have been about five years old, and my brother Josc about four. My brother and I were in a shopping cart and my grandfather was pushing the cart yelling—"Vendo gente" (I'm selling these kids). And my brother and I were laughing and asking him, "For how much?" And the prices would vary, but always ridiculous, like both for a penny. It was just lovely.

And my grandmother (Abuela Laura) was the same— a significant parent figure. She was feisty and a natural leader. She was the cook and laundry woman and fulfilled many of the domestic roles that my mother could not because she had become the breadwinner. Abuela Laura has this amazing green thumb and is like a *curandera* who can grow any type of herb and spice. When we get sick, she is the primary care provider and makes us *té de manzanilla* for colds and stomach ailments, or *baños de eucalipto* to clear the sinuses.

My grandmother was born in 1909, and we still depend on her for so many things—economic help, basic love advice, conflict mediation, and just unconditional love. My brothers, Mom, and I have realized that when we go to her home (she lives about five minutes by car from my mom), we all fall asleep. It is the ultimate refuge, and each and every one of us always ends up taking a nap because our bodies and souls are at such ease in her presence. It doesn't matter how well rested we are when we arrive, we will sleep profoundly and wake up feeling good, almost like when we were kids and took afternoon naps and woke up ready to play and eat and then play some more. That is what I feel like after a nap at my abuela's.

I feel incredibly lucky in the sense that my grandparents could afford economically and emotionally to be part of our lives. They came to the United States when we did. My mom is a single child and became part of the sandwich generation—caretaker to both children and parents. That may be an American concept. In Puerto Rico, these fluid caretaker roles are the norm and my grandparents assumed these roles beautifully. My grandparents were of a particular social class so that they had enough material resources to move and also to have their own housing. They always lived within one or two miles of us. As a kid and now as an adult, I know that we were their life, their reason to live, and their reason to hang in there. As my grandfather's life was ending, he would tell me, "I do not want to die. Who will take care of your mom, you, and your brothers?"

Family of Value

My definition of family is fluid and doesn't depend on blood. It goes beyond blood to people I really trust. I see myself raising my child in this network of people who will be aunts and uncles.

I am happy for the life I have been given. My parents raised beautiful sons and daughters and instilled in us a sense of duty, humility, and dignity. We love life and treat each other and others with gentleness. I know that I am loved, and this carries me every day.

Today

None of the four of us is married, and I don't think any of us sees ourselves getting married—at least for a long time. It's easier not to deal with that. Marriage is not necessary to have good relationships.

Do I want a partner? Yes, I want a partner. I also realize that it takes me a little longer to build an intimate relationship with a potential partner. My older brother and I hesitate when considering whether to go to the "permanent" stage in a relationship. For me it's about self-protection. It hurt a lot to allow people into my life and then have them disappear. Those disappearances occurred with our fathers.

Do I need a partner? No. I can be happy and complete without one. I also do not need one in order to have a family. A long-term relationship does not scare me. I think it would be a very beautiful thing to have—an intimate partner to share in day-to-day life, in raising a family, in the sensuousness of creating a home. The real question for me is can I create a home without a primary long-term relationship? And I think the answer is yes. I would be very scared if I thought I needed a partner in order to be happy and build a family. But at this point in my life, I do not see a partner as a prerequisite to the rest, and the rest is what is critical to me.

I always ask myself and the people I love—are you happy? The question of happiness has multiple dimensions, many at the same level of importance, and I do not place the issue of a primary long-term relationship at the forefront. There are other things of equal relevance, such as creating a collective that works on issues of social justice and creativity, building a family where I am the primary caregiver, and being able to support my friends as they build their own nuclear families.

I consider my brothers and myself to be incredibly independent and trustworthy people who can move quite easily into new situations. The stepfamily situation did not occur in a void—it occurred in multiple matrices of migration, acculturation, and education. My family is very rich in social capital.

Sophia's Advice for Stepparents

Allow the relationship to grow naturally.

Both stepfathers allowed intimacy to build between us slowly, the first by allowing me to partake in his world, the world of art. My mother and my older brothers expressed little interest in this. I on the other hand would spend many hours by his side seeing him draw, paint, carve wood, etc. Eventually as I expressed interest, he gave me access to his materials. I began to draw and paint. Later, with his encouragement, I applied and got into an art high school. I do not know if he knew the importance of his sharing this gift with me that I carry to this day. I felt that it was his gift to me, as I became his daughter. I bonded with him through art. It was ours alone. Critical in all this is that he did not force art on me. I went to him. He sensed that it was something that I liked and shared it with me as I expressed interest. He was smart that way—went slowly so that I never felt threatened or that he was forcing his way into my life as a father. He was a friend first; once I felt comfortable with him, he became a father figure.

Discipline comes later.

Stepchildren will act out—that's okay and, in fact, I would worry if they didn't act out. Think of this behavior as a challenge as the child adjusts to a new living environment. Consider carefully how you will handle discipline. I would not recommend a generic formula, but it helped me tremendously that my stepfather in the beginning was more of a friend than a parent. Regardless, when he did become a disciplinarian, it hurt like crazy, but it was easier to take because I had already built a positive relationship with him.

Sophia's Advice for Parents

Make sure your child feels loved and supported.

My advice depends on the age of the child. I think that a teenager who is becoming a stepchild will have different needs and wants than a small child. Regardless of the age, however, the child must feel loved and that the primary parent (the non-step one) will be present and supportive regardless of the pace in which intimacy is built within the "new" family unit.

Be aware of what the child has lost as a result of the new relationship. Yes, things are gained but there is also loss and there has to be a recognition of all that is encompassed in the stepchild-parent relationship.

Let intimacy develop naturally with the stepparent.

Intimacy is a difficult word to define, describe, or explain. It is basically the sense of belonging, of ease and comfort, of being home and not being conscious of how you look, what you say, how you may be perceived by those around you. When there is a new member in a family, one is acutely aware of self. When a new stepparent came into my life, I felt that I had lost the refuge of my home. I could no longer escape into the sweet and safe embrace of my home—it was now shared with someone I could not (albeit temporarily) trust. Even though my mom or dad said I could, I had to find out myself. Much of my acting out was, in fact, testing grounds to see if my mom still loved me, to see if this new person was willing to put up with me or push me aside.

My advice to parents is to go at the child's pace. Let him or her build intimacy with the stepparent on his or her own terms. This may take longer than expected. That's okay. I know that the times that I felt my mother was forcing time with my stepfather were also the times that I most resisted the new relationship. Let children give the stepparent the goodnight kiss when they are ready. They will do it when they feel it is right.

Also let the child and the stepparent spend time together alone, but do not force the issue either. I spent time doing art with my stepfather when I expressed interest in doing so. He never said "Sophia, come with me." I would just tag along and he would leave the door open or place pencils and paper in my sight. In any case, I got the hint that I was welcomed in the art studio and that I could come and go as I pleased. My mother also respected that space. She saw that time as ours and let the relationship flow on its own terms.

Sophia's Advice for Stepchildren

Seek out support systems.

What helped me a great deal was seeing other stepfamilies that were working. I was not the only stepchild in my circle of friends. My friends who were going though similar "step" adjustments played supportive roles. I was lucky because I was in an environment where support groups and open disclosure with friends were a fact of life. We talked about our feelings and growing up processes on a regular basis. For kids who do not have this supportive atmosphere, it is critical that the parents provide the tools and resources to help kids open up and disclose their feelings. This could mean a church group or a structured support group or even a camp. On a related note, our parents gave us the space necessary to hang out with our friends. I don't recall a curfew. As long as my mom knew that I was staying with my friends, she was okay. Many a late night we spent talking about our families.

Express yourself.

Talk about what you are feeling. My mom made a point of having "reuniones de familia" (family meetings) quite often. To this day, we all do it—if someone has identified an issue, a problem, or there is a fight in progress—any member of the family can call a meeting. We all have to drop what we are doing, meet in the living room, and talk it out. Let children call a meeting; let stepparents call a meeting. It fosters open dialogue.

■■■■■■■■■■■■■■■■■■■■■■■■■■■■■■■■

Errol

Errol is thirty-three years old. He has been married for four years and has a three-year-old daughter. He is a professional photographer and writer. Errol's parents divorced when he was four. His mother remarried twice; his father remarried once and is now, as Errol says, "finally in the process of getting that damned divorce." Errol has one half-sister and one distant stepbrother on his mother's side and two stepsisters on his father's.

Errol's Story

My conception of myself has never been as a step-child—but also, obviously, never as a child of a single unit family either. If anything, I was a child of my mother who raised me and there was this disconnect from my dad, even though he was there for me. So I was the child of two separate entities. A big success of my childhood was being able to evolve within the evolutions and revolutions of my "extended family."

My parents separated when I was somewhere between four and five, and I have no solid memories predating that split-up. Whatever rancor there was between my parents in their divorce was angry and ugly enough to shutter my mind to that epoch. Consequently, all the presumed happy time of my earliest life as we traveled around the world together is mostly lost to me. Growing up, I secretly identified with the character Tommy from The Who's rock opera of the same name. Having witnessed his father's murder by his stepfather, Tommy's "new family" roars at

him in chorus, "You never seen it, you never heard it..."
The scene is suffused with all the sweaty terror of grownups
being monsters to a pulpy child. In response to the trauma,
Tommy shuts down and seals off his mind. He sings si-
lently inside, "See me, feel me..." Though I was instead
loquacious and outgoing, I still bore the wounding of my
parents' divorce in a similar way. My tiny psyche blocked
out the storms of that period and locked them away with
the good stuff from before the tempest. I moved on, peace-
ably so, as if from a new starting point. This propensity to
cleave bad memories, and lose a few of the good with
them, has proved to be a standard of my emotional life.
All in all, though sometimes wasteful, this has probably
contributed to my being as perennially happy as I am....or
at least as "Buddhistically" in the moment as I tend to be.

I have a couple of postcard memories from my earliest childhood when, still united as a family, my parents
and I led a vivid life together, spending my first two years
in a windmill in Holland and then setting off across Nepal
and India. My memory banks contain exotic smells and
tastes, strange and awkward scales and mumbled languages
that I don't understand. But I have much clearer memories from a few years later when I would stare hard into
the mirror, fancying myself a young psychologist, succor-
ing dull hurt with congratulations that I could recognize
the complexities of Tommy's ordeal as bearing a resem-
blance to my own. My mom just thought I showed a young
and healthy inclination for rock 'n' roll. And let me prom-
ise you, rock 'n' roll has always helped too.

The Family, Extended and Otherwise

So my tango of love and antipathy that is the balanc-
ing act of thinking about one's parents while simultaneously
becoming a parent is built out of the garden/wrecking yard

of the once "broken," now "extended" family variety. I have this one beautiful early memory of going "movie-hopping" with my parents. The Santa Ana winds are blowing warmly, and the movie marquees are crisply bright. The sidewalk beneath me is smooth and swirling in dark polished stone. (However odious the street may be, Hollywood Boulevard will always be special to me.) I can remember having a parent at each hand swinging me. Never again in my life did I have my parents together holding my hands. Not until I took a picture of them sitting together holding my new daughter between them could I finally conceive of them as two people united by a child.

Instead, all through my youth I had the sense of them as people who belonged to both ends of my reality and who intermittently came together in the same room on my behalf. That's a pleasantry I took for granted early on because my mom always put the kids first. For many years, family functions included both parents and their extended broods all gathered around Mom's table and it never seemed like much of a hassle. My sister and I have different fathers, and even though her father was relatively quick to be "extended" from my mother, still the holidays brought everyone together as a mini-society. At best, or at least, Christmas Eve served as the microcosm of the spread-out family system; contiguous while being many layered and all these layers laced together with strange and unique fillings squished between. True to the late twentieth-century urban/urbane mold it was "A Room Full of Family."

I have a million reasons to despise my stepmother but Christmas Eve has always been one of the best. The more she took to drink, the more she fucked with Christmas. She would always make a scene, would always get sloppy, would always have to be physically removed at the end of the night by my embarrassed father. I didn't recognize my mother's crippling sadness over it until I was older and my mother was more willing to confide in me such things. But my father's embarrassment hit an early primal chord of compassion in me. I wanted to pull to me this man who was being pulled away. It gave me my own first taste of paternal worry. My father was chucking his stab at fatherhood in lieu of nursing this woman and her demons. I didn't want him to lose me as much as I didn't want to lose him.

Through my teen years, my dad wasn't much at those family functions anymore. It was too painful for the *grownups.* The kids just lost out and I had to do holidays twice, once with this family, and once again with the other. So I lost forever that childhood grail of the two people being in my life simultaneously. They were both there for me theoretically and practically, and Mom saw to it that they were never more than a few minutes drive apart, and I'll always be thankful for that, but there was always that subcutaneous weight of "choosing" between them. Nevertheless, my mom really raised me. I don't have a sense of being a stepchild, but a child of my mom and then all these parental appendages trailing behind that primary identity.

Both my parents remarried people who were midgets compared to them, psychologically and intellectually. I have a sense that my parents gravitated to these people as an antidote to whatever rigors they had put each other through. My parents are both large, forceful personalities, and their new mates were obviously the easy way out. I have anger towards all my stepparents for how they came in and, victims of their own shattered childhoods, fed at the tit of my parents' parenthood. I think of them much more as stepchildren than as stepparents.

My Father's House

My biological dad was the satellite character whom I saw on Wednesday nights and Saturdays. *Charlie's Angels* and *Fantasy Island* on one visit, cartoons and pancakes on the other. As my stepmother became a more constant factor in his life, I, by the same measure, pulled away. She was mean and I didn't like being around her, even if that meant spending less time with my dad.

My stepmother was a very young woman when my dad took up with her. She had no education and no vocation other than waitressing in Hollywood. She was a basket case. She had nothing to offer to her own three children, much less to me. She was as much her daughter's sister as her mother. I doubt you could say she was ever really her *parent*. We never got along. My anger towards my stepmother revolves around her simply being there. She insinuated herself into my dad's world, and I started going there less and less.

Besides treading on my turf, her curtness and threats of violence made the family they were creating a scary place to be. I had never been hit in my life, and the moment she first raised her hand to threaten me—I must have been all of six—I knew this person had no real authority but was only a bully. The hate began in earnest, half out of misunderstanding, half out of self-preservation. I couldn't tie the notion of motherhood to this woman, who thrashed and belittled her kids and allowed them to sleep on the service porch. By the time they bought a house together, she had her claws in enough to make sure that none of us got our own rooms. Disenchanted with the foldout couch, I really let go of the notion of having my own place in my dad's world. I can remember one night asking politely if I might use the phone. As it came out of my mouth, it broke both our hearts. I was a fucking guest in my father's home.

For the entirety of the twenty-five years they lived

together in that house, I can see her working her way in endless circles from soap operas on the idiot box, to the booze chest, and to the stove where'd she'd prepare these huge plates of spaghetti bolognaise that she thought Italian men would appreciate. "How's that sauce, huh?" she'd cajole and threaten in that awful cigarette wheeze. Like a billion other rotten parents, my stepmother's malaise was stoked by drink and daytime serial drama. She pursued no goals and seemed to have given up on fostering dreams. Where's the pith in being a housewife whose children hate you and whose husband works chronically late to avoid you? She took my dad not only away from me but also from his whole Italian family. It was that same embarrassment. Poker at his brother's house had even become a bummer. She only got worse over the years as she pruned in her bath of alcoholism and monotony. My dad, lost in his own Italian/chivalric guilt and the unresolved issues of his own long-dead but always cold and distant mother, hung on, enabling where he thought he was helping, claiming to be observant of his manly duties to his wife. Manly duties he had rather blithely foregone with my mom, I kept thinking.

After years of failed interventions and the whole family gently urging him to realize that her self-destructive verve was taking its toll on his own health, he finally began to get the picture. On the day my daughter was born, he could barely hold her because he was so stricken with fatigue and shingles. It became apparent that rather than nursing his ills, this vindictive woman was killing him. He began to catch on to the paradigm he was trapped in, and as his strength returned, so did some resolve. Before the year was over, he had moved her into her own apartment.

I believe that the one thing that really let him sever ties with her totally was seeing the fantastic marriage I have with my wife and the diamond of bliss that our child is as she sits between us. I like to think that I have given my father the glimpse of an archetype that his father couldn't give him and that he in turn couldn't show me: a view of man and woman as husband and wife really being equals and really building a life in tandem, that is to say, having a family.

In my twenties I feel I regained my father. We restructured our relationship of father and son. We rebuilt it by devoting solid time to doing things together. We got to know each other better and, for the past decade, Thursday has been our dinner night and we rarely miss it. And it's been wonderful because I have been able to heal one of the great hurts of my life, that of not having a father. It's the Great American Syndrome—the mom raises the kids, and everyone has this great respect and empathy for their mom, but they want their daddy, the daddy that didn't exist. Be it Willy Lowman or just plain Divorced Dad, the lack of mentor keeps things from ever working very well. In the past ten years, we've been able to put our relationship back together through conscious decision and straightforward effort. We have resurrected our father-son relationship primarily by hanging out together, making the effort and making the time, and little by little, teaching each other about ourselves, how we are made of the same mold. Now of course I'm busier; I'm the full-time father. We still make our once-a-week dinner though. But now he says, "Are you bringing the kid? Because I gotta see the kid." And on Sundays she devours his pancakes.

He now has a girlfriend who is a peer and friend to him. It's terrific to see him beaming in the springtime of his old age. I recently remodeled his kitchen for him, and it was a soulful experience. I spent days alone working at his house. Sometimes I had my daughter and wife there with me, but no stepmother. I got to enjoy the place finally and to wipe away the imprint of that woman. I gave him back his kitchen, the heart and hearth of the place, done in his own image, but with me as the crafter of that image. I built a place for myself in my father's house.

My Mother's House

My mom was in her early thirties when she divorced my father. She had been orphaned as a child so she had no proper family structure to fall back on. She had resources though. She had her self-esteem. She knew how to cook and how to make magic in anyone's kitchen. She had garnered a knowledge of exotic cooking from our travels around the world and she turned this into a successful catering business that did all the big "mealing and dealing" parties in the Hollywood hills of the 70's. That's how she supported us. She also had her network of friends from the 60's who were our extended family proper. Their kids grew up with us as cousins and brothers and sisters. Having had no one by blood, she pulled to her as family the people she really wanted to have there. And maybe her most sterling resource was her ability to put a silver lining into everything. The cares of adults were well shielded from us. We just knew our dads were not in the immediate scenario and it was mostly left to that.

Our mom was a rock for us, and we were the river that flowed all around her. She is a really creative, expansive, loving person. She was the one who always made everything a party. She raised us without a religion but with an embrace of spirituality, Eastern thinking, and appreciation. She would always have big holiday parties and everybody was invited. Anybody in town who didn't have a family for the season wound up on our doorstep. Mom had memories of a rotten childhood, so she went out of her way to make our childhoods wonderful and fanciful. We never had much money but we never knew it. We traveled and we played and there were always lots of presents under the tree. Life was ensconced in allegories and make-believe and for us as kids that was enough.

Virgil was my first stepfather. My childhood memories pretty much begin with Virgil being in the house. He is my sister's father and she is six years my junior. My mom and he never married, so there was no celebration or coronation of him entering the scene as a father figure. He was just there as far as I can remember. They set up a pretty neat household together, filled with Pop Art and handsome antiques. That early exposure to good art has had a huge impact on my life, and it's a legacy of aesthetic appreciation for which I will always be indebted to Virgil.

Virgil was old enough and sage enough to carry some father stature. He was enough of a man to be a contender, but he was far from being *responsible* enough to become a father figure. He didn't really adopt me in any way. He was just a fuck-up. So even though I was young enough to be open-hearted about the whole thing, I was already wise enough not to take too much stock in him. I'm sure my mom was attracted as much by the wounded boy in him as by the rakish, worldly man he presented.

Wilbur, my second stepfather, comes in when I'm twelve and he was all of twenty at most. He was very much a boy still, a weltered pup and the product of successive stepfathers who had beaten him while his mother looked on. He was, and remains to this day when off his medication, a violently angry person. He brought that anger into our house. He brought yelling into our home and it was rotten. Screaming room to room and punching holes in the walls were things we just didn't have up till then. All of a sudden, instead of having a new father figure, my sister and I felt that Mom had adopted an abandoned child with insurmountable troubles and whose tortured soul came before ours. "Why is there another hole in the wall?"

we'd wonder in the morning. All of a sudden he came first because he needed parental understanding more than we did. And though we tried our best to dispute this with our mom, her god-given gift for care-giving took over and superseded her better judgment.

Wilbur was primarily a troubled asshole with a nice streak. He was dyslexic and so largely illiterate. Owing to his youth and lack of education, he had no profession beyond fringe Hollywood extra, bouncer, stuntman for a day, car salesman. We would come home and he would be doing his newest hobby like train-building or kite-making on the kitchen table. "Mom, who is this guy?" Nobody's ever really understood Mom's connection to him. She's such an interesting and intelligent woman she could have found any manner of worthy peer. I never bought her bullshit about all the good ones having died in 'Nam. I knew exactly why Wilbur stayed: you can't turn out the stray once you've taken him in. Now at forty he's really come into himself. He's fat, balding, and ashen with chronic back pain.

Wilbur brought a cloud to the little family unit we were eking by with. It was the family unit of the future, these awkward nuclei that are not based on tradition but on function. And my mom and sister and I had had some real harmony. He was the bull that huffed his way into our menagerie. I'll never forgive him that trespass. He fucked with our music; he was alien to harmony of any kind. As I get older, I begin to forgive him. He didn't know any better. He was a downtrodden person from the get-go. He wanted that enlightenment and good mommy-ing of our mother as much as we did. Affording him that understanding didn't mean I had to like him though. And I certainly didn't want people thinking I was related to him. He had nothing to offer as a father figure, and yet no matter how many times I told him not to do it, I'd still run into people who would say, "I met your father...." and I'd have to explain that no, he was definitely not my father, and that perplexed look on their face would fall away. The place of My Father was a very tender issue, and he still refuses to be bright or understanding enough to respect that. In return, my respect for him has remained in the smidgen category and vacillates up and down from there.

Wilbur has stepped up to the plate as far as being "grandpa" and gets many points for doting on my daughter. It's that teddy-bear side of him that just wants to love and be loved in return. Had there not been twenty years of mediocre to bad blood between us, I'd probably be able to extend him more congeniality.

I still feel particularly hurt by the fact that Mom never wanted to hear our protests against Wilber. Or anyone else's for that matter. She never seemed to side with us. And then all of a sudden, he would be gone and she would say a few rotten things about him and good riddance. We'd wait respectfully for her to mention that we had been right. But she wouldn't and, of course, he would come back. Where else was he going to go? He had never grown up. So it was back to Mom, our mom. We were the ones who finally grew up and left.

A focal point of relating to Mom now is having her involved with my daughter. My chick is a born princess and to have a fairy grandmother built in is just perfect. The glow they share together is beautiful to watch. They really admire each other. My mother's dharma is to mother and now to be able to give her that opportunity again seems like a fitting tribute to a woman who has always given so selflessly to me.

Siblings

My sister is six years younger. Our relationship was

really close as we grew up. Despite the difference in age, we were allies. She was precious. My own child is not the first baby I cared for; I proudly changed my sister's diapers. It was my first big contribution to the household, to help care for my baby sister when my mom was scrambling hard to care for us. My sister's father was largely out of the picture long before she was out of diapers. So there was the trio of us, and then these satellite fathers that made up the basis of our extended family. When I left for college, she felt terribly left behind. I had been her primary father figure, and she was left with only Wilber and the nubbin of her own father.

Virgil had a son by a previous marriage who was a few years older than I, and we were close when we were young. But his mother was a real mind- and ball-buster. He was imaginative and sophisticated and seemed to get along well despite his circumstances. I felt sorry for him that he didn't have a mom as cool as mine. By the time he was a teenager, Virgil's son had pretty much removed himself from his father's life, which meant he was out of my sister's and my life too. It turns out he spent most of his entire high school career stoned on acid and then finally came to terms with himself and married a Marine, a guy who was the very picture of the tough guy Virgil had always wanted his son to be.

There was never a compelling emotional bond built between my stepmom's brood and me. They were made in the image of their evil mother. The older sister had been a drug addict and runaway since she was eleven, so she wasn't much in the picture. There was a son who lived with his father. He didn't like his mom.

The youngest daughter and I were the same age. She was cute, I was cute, we were supposed to get along famously. We despised each other. She pushed my buttons relentlessly. She taught me the depths of my own budding

Italian anger. I hadn't tasted that yet in my life, and it was way too powerful. I recognized right away that it wasn't healthy to truck in such violent emotions. She in the meantime was being taught that that was the only way to get attention. She has always been a very smart person, but thanks to her terrible upbringing, she hasn't done a thing with her life. She's never held down a job or had a lasting relationship. We became friends in our twenties, and she would often regale me with horror stories about her experience growing up as a stepchild. My father never embraced her, never provided the father figure she needed. That was all part of that weird world I had pulled away from. She would tell me these things to try and push my buttons again, but I had largely grown past all that. We remained friends despite her amazing pathology. She would, without fail, turn on anyone who tried to love her. It was her way of confirming her un-lovability. She would antagonize with every tooth in her head just to prove that the person never really cared in the first place. She would try it with me over and over, and I'd laugh it off. But then she tried it with my wife and I had to draw the line. I couldn't entertain her sickness in the sphere of my own fledgling family. She's since moved to Paris and taken up with a married man to try and build some sort of family of her own. Like her brother and her sister before her, she's cut any familial ties to her mother. I have no relationship with her now.

Today I am who I am.

As far as how this erratic childhood has affected my life, what do I know about my legacy and myself? One thing I do have is a sense of what's at stake if my marriage were to be lost. That's not a fantasy, not some fanciful thing to rationalize. It's a great pain I've worn across my

forehead since childhood. When my wife and I fight, sometimes she'll say, "So, do you want a divorce?" It's just her
way of saying, "Fuck you." I always stop her and tell her,
"You can't even joke like that, because it means nothing
to you but it means everything to me." I tell her, if she
wants to push my buttons, she's really doing it by saying
that and, lo, remember the Italian anger. It strikes a deep
cord with me that it doesn't with her. She can be offhanded
about it because it isn't a reality to her. Her parents would
never divorce. It would be like cutting off limbs from one
body.

Recently I was looking at a photograph of my wife's
parents. For me to witness a family unit that has been together all these years, the picture of young mother and
father on the mantle, the same two people who are old
mother and father together—it's heartening and compelling to me. My mother provided the grand notion of us as
this gypsy band, but the united front of the One Family
was always the other fairy tale. My in-laws give me a peri-
scope into the world of a man and woman who have gone
through life together and done the things of life together,
had careers, had children, built houses, traveled and
travailed, and now get to dote on the grandkids. They
weren't torn apart by drugs, they weren't undone by sexual
revolution, or madness, or depression, or the nagging notion they could find something better. Now near the end
of their lives, they still have each other.

And I also learned something totally fucking pristine
about family from my mother. It was something she learned
by being an orphan. Families are the people you take to
you and make as your family. I learned that family is the
people who you hold close to your heart and not necessarily the people you popped out of. Although I came from
this split-up family, I never felt I came from dysfunction.
That's important to me and to what I own as my child-

hood. With lots of love balming everything over, we were always very functional. We worked. I am an optimist, and I will make my family work.

Errol's Advice for Stepparents

See the situation through the child's eyes.

When parents break up, it introduces the child to the notion of parents as something far less than eternal. How can a child grasp the idea that their first point of reference is now two points? It is a stellar calamity, and stars do fall right out of the sky. And if the earth doesn't open up and swallow the child, then that child is left to walk a new landscape of broken glass and instability. Nothing is as it was before. Are mommies still mommies? It's terribly frightening. It's a big deal. It's THE big deal. Then to try and fathom a new parent coming in, that's the admission of a broken god. Stepparents must have some empathic vision of what the child is experiencing.

Don't replace the parent, but be parent-like.

For a small kid, the parent has to explain—"Here is a person who is going to be a stepfather, daddy two, not your father. You have a father and he is not going away." You have to make things black and white, simpler. "This person is not going to replace your mommy or daddy. But this new person is here for you too. He/she will love and protect you and be there for you." Then the stepparent has to chime in, "I know that you have a real daddy or mommy and I know they're right over there and I'll never interfere with that. That's none of my business. But if you're ever angry at your mommy or daddy, you can come to me and we'll go to the movies."

In the case of an adolescent child, it's the opposite of

black and white. You have to set up an open, ongoing dialogue. "I am coming into your house, and I understand that it is your house." This is especially important with a male child and a stepfather. There is a supplanting of authority and the man of the house position must be shared, not usurped.

In either case, the trick is, you don't try to be a father; instead you are a parental figure, i.e., a responsible party, a compassionate, understanding yet authoritative person. You should be "father-like" yet dispassionately removed. Available yet not intrusive. The stepparent must be very careful about treading on the territory of parental identity and must carve out a new niche, the stepniche.

Develop your own relationship with your stepchild.

Don't move in too quickly. Allow the relationship to develop. For any young person and adult to get along, there has to be some kind of bonding. The child needs to feel that they have a one-on-one relationship with the adult in order to feel safe and free with them. Let the new stepparent develop a rapport independently with the child, as well as within the family setting. If there is an issue, the real parent doesn't have to always be the arbitrator. The stepparent can thereby become a resource to the "original" family as opposed to just an adjunct to it.

I don't remember ever bonding with my stepmother. I rode in her broken-down red Camero maybe once. Virgil, my stepfather, took us to the movies and museums, and I had a much better relationship with him. I can remember his white Mustang, as beat up as that Camero, but much friendlier and inviting. When he lived in our house, he didn't seem so out of place; he wasn't an intruder but an addition. Bonding is sharing something simple yet enduring that sets up a glue between two people.

Expect to be rejected.

Stepparents are most likely going to be rejected at first, and they have to stay Buddha-like about it. No attachment. Don't take it personally. Be a grownup. My dad could have waited for his stepkids to warm up to him by being a good guy, by being an adult. But instead, everything was forced and everything stayed broken.

The primary thing about stepparenting is that you cannot force it on a child. Offer it up; let the child make the choice. Just as you don't force friendship upon the friends of your child. You can be affable and parental and then slyly win them over with wiles. You have to offer the child the opportunity to see that strength can be garnered, help can be won, and security can be had; they need only gravitate toward you. If, as a stepparent, you can provide that godfatherly sense of "I am a new sanctuary for you," the winning over might be very simple. It might take little more than a full tank of gas and a ready $20 for the movies. In a child's world, it's the simple moments of poetry that count.

Errol's Advice for Parents

Put your child first.

What do we want for our kids? Very simply we want them to be happy; we want them to be healthy and wise. How can you put yourself before them? If you learn the great lesson of parenting, it's selflessness. If you break up and start over, you have to remember that your children are part of the equation. You must not encumber them with the jabs and needles of your own crapped-out self-esteem. They are just beginning to grasp the fact that lives can break and mend again.

If you are going to invite someone in to be a parental figure, you had better be damned well sure they're going to be a real parental figure. Young people appreciate parents. They don't want flunkies coming into their house.

The biological parent has to remember to not take sides with the new spouse, even if they're right. The parent must be neutral or just plain take the kid's point of view, right or wrong. It's called solidarity. The kid needs to know that you as the parent understand what they are going through. You must be there for them. The Rock.

And if you see your children infrequently, spend the time with them exclusively. If you're only going to see me twice a week, spend time with me and only me. Lavish me with attention. Share your world, but also share mine.

Communicate as a family.

If you're going to remarry and do a Brady bunch scenario—and especially if you have an adolescent—you must have United Nations dialogues. Great summits must be held, but monologues must be banned. You need to *listen* to your child. Nothing can be an ultimatum. The forge must be stoked and prodded or you'll never make new metal.

Don't put the other parent down.

It's definitely not healthy. There is no need for it. Separated parents fighting through their children should expect to see every personal failing magnified tenfold in the flesh of their progeny.

Be the adult.

You're going to have heartache. Somehow you put a happy face on it. There's room for about five minutes of self-pity and wallowing when you're bringing up a child. You must get off your ass and stick to the work at hand.

If you're going to have a "band-aid" relationship, don't force it upon your children. Compartmentalize if need be, but guard the sanctity of the "original" family. If you are going to marry someone because you have found a more proper mate, then count yourself blessed, but remember that parents are the responsible parties and children are the parties who are learning responsibilities, not the other way around.

Errol's Advice for Stepchildren

Take a pro-active role.

How do you overcome the hardship of living with other people? You listen. You try to work with the people you live with. You try to get along. My information to the adolescent is that you may be the smartest person involved. Maybe you're the one that has to be the diplomat and make conversation. Maybe you're the one who has to facilitate the fact that, "Hey, you're bringing someone into my house, *my* house, not their house. Just because you brought them in doesn't make it theirs. I have lived here my whole life and you want to invite someone else in? What if I brought another teenager here to live? Wouldn't you feel a tad tread upon?" You have to be involved in the concession-making process. I believe that families that work well only do so because everyone is pro-actively involved.

■■■■■■■■■■■■■■■■■■■■■■■■■■■■■■■■■■

Sebastian

Sebastian is thirty years old. His parents, who were never married, separated by the time he was two. His step-father, who had been with his mother previously, recon-nected with his mother shortly after. He is one of seven siblings from three fathers. Four are half-siblings from his mother's first husband. One is his half-brother from his mother's second husband, and he has a sister from his father and mother. He has been in a committed relation-ship for the past eleven years, and is the first person in his family to graduate from college. He is a union orga-nizer.

Sebastian's Story

Trying to figure out when I became a stepchild is complicated because my mom actually met my stepdad before she met my dad. She had my sister and myself with my dad. They had an off-and-on relationship for a year or two, and then my stepdad came back into the picture. So I would say I became a stepchild when I was one or two years old. My mom and stepdad divorced two or three times over the years, but they're still together. My dad never remarried.

We had one house in Phoenix, Arizona. Initially my dad lived there, and then right after he moved out, my stepdad moved in. We stayed there until I was seven or eight years old, and then we started moving back and forth between this house and my grandmother's house. The last time I remember living at my grandmother's house, it was really crowded. It was my mom, grandmother, sister, two brothers, and several uncles. There were just so many people. It was always back and forth. Literally, in one year we would move five to seven times from my nanna's house to my mom's. My father lived in a really small, small apartment about two miles away from us. It was next door to a bar, so he was mostly at the bar. Whenever we'd visit, we'd visit him at the bar. He was never at his home.

When I was fourteen, I wanted out of this situation. I got a job at McDonald's and rented a trailer that was close to my work. It was my own house, my own trailer. I lived there, I bought clothes, I paid rent, I went shopping, I gave my mom money, and I've worked ever since. My mom told me recently that I am the only one of her sons who has never given her problems. I was never around. I have never asked her for anything since I was fourteen.

Stepdad

My stepfather Antonio was originally from Chihuahua, Mexico. He had a wife and kids there. And, like a lot of Mexican males, he came to the U.S. to make money and move back. But he came here, met my mom, and maybe he intended to go back, but he never did. So he abandoned his whole family—his parents, his wife, and his children. He never saw them again, never went back. He was short and chubby with a big belly, always cracking jokes and listening to Banda music. He had a lot of energy, very robust, and was good with women. They liked him.

I think I loved him as a child. I wanted a dad, like all kids. I needed to have him as a dad. I really tried. He was the only man around. Early on he tried to be a father. But it didn't work. When he was sober, it was fine. Once he would drink, it was completely over. I mean he was aggressive, mean, and violent. He might have hit my mom on a few occasions. Mostly he just screamed and yelled. I remember once sitting at a table and listening to him apologize to me, but come Friday, regardless of apologies, he would get paid, and then there would be fights. I have all these memories of being afraid of him, climbing out of windows at night, running away, going to my grandma's or an aunt's house, hiding in closets—you name it.

The worse thing my stepdad did is that he molested my two youngest siblings and me. This came back to me when I was about seventeen-years old. I remember that I was reading the Bible (back then I was a Christian), and this overwhelming sadness came over me. I began to remember bits and pieces of a horrible dream. I started to cry and realized that I was not making this up; it did happen. I had completely forgotten about it along with many other incidences that involved people who wanted to hurt me. I will never understand how someone could hurt a kid that was just trying to survive. I think I'm over it, and then sometimes I remember. And I wonder why, if my mom knew about it, she would have allowed it. Was she lonely? I can even make excuses for her—she only had a second-grade education; her parents mistreated her. But still she did not protect me. I told my mom, my grandmother, and my sister about it, but they didn't do anything. They told me to go to bed with no dinner. And that was the end; I never had a memory of it again. Recently I called my sister and asked her why so many people were mean to me. She told me that she remembered that night. She remembers me coming home crying and telling them about the abuse. I wasn't sure I had told them. I thought maybe I had kept it a secret. But I did tell them, and they told me to go to bed.

We always knew that we had a real dad; we knew that our stepdad wasn't our real dad. But I even think that we would have accepted him had he not been so abusive. I remember feeling" I want to love you, but I know you're going to hurt me." At some point, I stopped loving him. It hurts to try and explain who he was.

I do have a few good memories of my stepdad. My mom had apartments, and he and I would fix them together. It was nice to hold the board when he sawed something. But so much negativity overruled the niceness and the loving-him part. He was here recently helping me build a house, and it was so hard sitting looking at this man thinking, "You're it, you're the one. You're like my dad but you have caused me so much pain, so much anxiety." It was weird to have him here because I was wrestling with my own issues with him. A part of me felt like I wanted to love him because he's an old man now. I wanted to connect with him, but I'm just like, "No, you were so bad." And ironically, my mom recently divorced him. Out of the blue. And I felt bad for him. How could my mom do this? She's leaving him now when he's a broken man. He's disabled, he can't do anything, and now she leaves him. He's been my dad. I mean he is my dad, and yet today as I am helping him with his citizenship papers, I wonder, "Why am I helping this guy?" I have absolutely no real connection with him. Absolutely no connection.

There were also cultural barriers. There is a difference between a Chicano kid and a Mexican male. I am American-born, Mexican American. He is a Mexican man. In Mexico the father is definitely the boss, the man of the house, the patriarch. I grew up with my mom as the boss. My mom is the one I respect. This created a conflict because he felt that he needed to be right. I didn't have that feeling. He knew that even though we had it poor, it was not as poor as in Mexico. He felt, "Look kid, you're all right. You've got this; you've got that." He might have been thinking about his kids who had it worse because they were in Mexico. We had little food, but they had no food.

Dad

My biological dad was never around, never, never around. He fought in World War II when he was really young, and then in the Korean and Vietnam Wars. He had four wounds from where he had been shot. So he was disabled, and he had a limp. And of course, he had all the psychological scars, so he really stayed away. He never came over to the house. He wasn't a dad that would pop by and say, "Hey, you know, I want to see my kids." He never did that.

I was really depressed this year on Father's Day because I always wanted to love my dad but couldn't. There was just no relationship. I saw him always at a bar. Sometimes we would get a booth. We would drink Shirley Temples, hang out, and he would show us off to all of his bar patron friends, all very drunk people. And we'd stay for maybe twenty minutes and then we'd leave. That was our total visit. That was the only place that I visited him. As a kid I kind of liked it. It was kind of fun, loud, a lot of people. It didn't dawn on me until later how odd it was. I remember one time we had pulled up to see him, and he was actually sleeping in the oleanders next to the bar. He had just been run over by a car. His leg was run over and it was dramatic; he was in pain. You know it's hard to think that your father's a bum and he's sleeping in the oleanders. It's a tough memory.

He was always drinking. He had so much pain. We would visit him two or three times a year, Father's Day and Christmas and maybe one or two other times. We stopped visiting him when I was eleven or twelve, and after I moved out at fourteen, I never went to visit him. The last time I visited was in 1992, and he died shortly after. I stare at his picture now and think about how he died, a lonely man in a really awful apartment building, gross and falling apart. But I know he really did love my sister and me.

These are my only memories of my dad. I'm trying to grow into a healthy adult and these things affect you. When you are a child, who makes you feel that you are worth something, who makes you feel important?

Mom

My mom was brought up in a dysfunctional family in a very small village in Phoenix. Back then it was like a village. She had a second-grade education. She picked cotton with my grandmother. I have to give her credit for that. I'm the baby of the family, and I got a lot of love from my mom. I think she did help boost my self-esteem and made me think that I could do something. She spent every other Sunday exclusively with me. She would take me to get an ice cream and show me rich people's homes. That little bit of attention made me want to go forward and do better. She made me ambitious. I've always been pretty ambitious.

There are seven kids in my family, four sons and three daughters. My mom stopped being a mom when I was five or six. She went to parties, drank, and went out with my dad or stepdad. I don't really have recollections of her being a bad mom or a negative mom. I still have a good relationship with her. I really love her. She's the only thing I have.

I'm now coming to grips with the fact that my mom was a selfish woman who made very unwise decisions. All her husbands were losers; every one of them was an alcoholic. She was only married to one of them, the first one. That's when she was the epitome of a great wife and she did everything right. I give her some credit that she tried her hardest with the one husband. She had four kids, worked her butt off, and it just ended badly. So I think maybe she thought, "I've done everything. Why not be a party wife too?" She got fed up with it.

My mom and stepdad would fight all the time. There were all these screaming matches. A typical night would be—we're at home; we're in bed; he comes home; they fight. She either hides us under the bed or in a closet. Or she tells my big brother, "Take them and leave; go run to Nana's house." My childhood was always running from place to place. We'd run to my grandma's house and he'd follow. He'd be banging on the door, coming in, and we were calling the police and hiding in closets. And that was my whole childhood.

Brothers, Sisters, and Grandma

I have five half-siblings and one full sibling. My mom married her first husband Roland, and they had Rene, Sam, Ana and John. She was married to him for many years. He was also an alcoholic. Her second boyfriend was Ed and they had one kid named Cade. Third is my dad Harold, and they had two kids, my sister Anastia and me. Ironically, my mom had seven kids with white men and no kids with my stepdad, who's Mexican. So we're all half; we're mixed.

We all grew up together; my brothers and sisters were there for me, but they were a lot older than me. I'm thirty now, my oldest sister must be forty-six, and then my sister right above me is thirty-one. The people who raised me were Rene and Ana. They both took me in and tried to help me. They are doing really well in their lives. My brother John had a serious learning disability. Sam is the most dysfunctional. He ended up in prison.

Sam tried to take on a dad role and beat up on me a lot. He knows that. He feels guilty about it. He didn't know how to be a dad. He shouldn't have been a parent. He was too young. My two brothers got into gangs and ended up in prison, one of them for five years, the other one was in and out of jail. They were tattooed up and down. They were like the rough guys.

My two older sisters really resent my mom because they were there and they know what happened. They had their childhoods taken from them because they had to watch us while she was at the bar or hanging out, especially my sister Ana. She is still watching over me. She still coaches me. She is definitely a mom to me. I really care for her.

My sister Anastia and I are very close. Biologically we have the same dad. But I think it's not just the dad thing. We grew up together. We were together all the time. She is really quiet, very soft-spoken, but she has an incredible temper. She actually fought a lot of my battles as a kid. She beat up everybody that came my way, boys and girls. She's really, really tough. She fought grown women. If anybody said anything to me, she would be there beating them up. I'm really, really super close with her.

My little brother Cade and I got along all right, but we grew up with animosity because he was a privileged kid. It's a skin color dynamic. He was like "the white kid." I mean, he's completely white. He doesn't look Mexican at all. My grandmother and aunts really spoiled him. He was always taken away from the house because he was a cherished kid, and my sisters and I were left alone.

I had a hard relationship with my grandmother because she had to put up with us. My grandma was really aggressive toward me. She had her deadbeat sons living with her, and she had my mom and her kids. And then occasionally my aunt's kids would be there too. So there was a houseful of kids. And it was crazy. I mean, it was really, really crazy and chaotic. I feel that my grandma was a good woman, but she had nine kids and an abusive, alcoholic husband. She left her husband and toughed it out on her own. I think because she had left her husband, she thought, "I did it, so you can too." And my mom basically never did.

My grandma was a very, very, very hard woman, very, very stern. And I was a hyperactive kid. I mean I was hyperactive. She never liked me. She was always hitting me. There was a lot of abuse. We were in her house, adding to her stress. I would talk back, I was rough; I was mean, and she made me pay for it. I don't blame her.

Now my grandmother is ninety-some years old. I graduated from college in 1995, and today I'm the best thing in the world to her. All the other grandkids are, you know, working at a toyshop or what not, and I'm the pride and joy. But it wasn't that way back then. Today I have a pretty good relationship with her.

Now

The whole stepchild experience has affected my life. I'm afraid at night. When I'm lying in bed thinking about the next day, if there's a test, school, work, I mean, whatever it is, I'm just overwhelmed with fear. And I always wonder, why am I so afraid right now? At the house where I grew up, bad things happened at night.

I am sometimes cold in my relationships, distant. I don't like people to be very loving with me. I just don't like it. I can hug people and say, "How are you?" It's more a love thing. If my partner really loves me, I don't like it. There's an inability to connect there. I don't want to connect on that level. I don't want to be all very hunky-dory happy. It makes me feel weird, freaked out. Don't hug me and be all happy. You can hug me, but if you get excited and like "Oh I love you, love you, love you," I just can't do it. My mom never had that kind of relationship with my stepdad, so I've never really seen it.

I can understand the whole gamut of people's emotions—the sadness, the crying, the heartache, and the pain. And I just instinctually know how I can help. It's just natural, because I've been there. There's a little kid I have right now at work that reminds me of myself. He's hyperactive, he won't sit still, he talks back, and he's aggressive. I can just imagine what his life is like. My manager's saying, "Kick him out of the program. You don't need that; don't make it hard on yourself." But I say, "Why do you want to kick him out? Where's he going to go?" Two weeks ago, something happened; the kid got upset because I made him switch bikes. They have to share the new bikes, because there are new and old bikes. Well, he got upset and he ran off. His dad came screeching around the corner, all drunk, and he's yelling and screaming at me. I couldn't say to the boy, "Your dad's a drinker" or "You've got issues at home" but I knew.

I'm totally, totally, totally at risk for becoming an alcoholic, because it's generational, starting with my stepdad, my dad, my grandfather, my brothers, everybody. I know that I would definitely have a drinking problem if I let myself go. So I have to tell myself, "You just can't do it."

My concept of family is different now. My family here is Ray and I and his sisters. Growing up, I didn't really know what family was. I moved to Maine around 1990 to live with my sister. She would have dinner on the table and I hated it. I just couldn't stand being at a table and having dinner. It felt so weird to me. And she was saying, "You come over here and you sit down." It was so foreign to me to sit down at a table and everybody's got a plate and they've got utensils. And it was just awful. It took me a long time to get used to that. We never did that as a family. I think dinner says it all for a lot of families. It's your chance to sit down and talk about what's going on. It's good stuff. I think that my perception of family was definitely distorted.

As I got older, I would see healthy families and think, "Wow, that is so nice, I wonder what it's like to do that," because we just didn't have that. It was not there. Nothing of the sort was there. My concept of family now is really just hanging out with the people you like and love, people you enjoy being around. I think my favorite thing is to hang out on the sofa and watch movies, and be together that way, rather than hang out at dinner tables. That's my favorite thing to do for a family affair.

What I'd like my parents to know about me today varies from moment to moment. Sometimes I want them to know that it's been hard, really, really hard. I'm thirty years old, a man now. But sometimes I still feel like a kid, worthless, really, really sad. I just wonder why people decide to have kids. Don't have kids if you're not going to love them, and don't have kids if they have to be brought up the way I was brought up. I almost didn't make it. I could have been a dead kid. I could have been in prison.

On a positive level, sometimes it can work out. Despite all that negativity, something has caused me to be lucky. I am happy to be alive now. I think my life is going well. I'm the only family member who has drive, who wants to change things.

Sebastian's Advice for Stepparents

Be the adult.

There's a kid here. He might be horrible, but he is still a kid. You need to try harder. You be the adult, whether you are twenty-one or forty. If you can't be the adult, you're better off being single. If you are going to be jealous or confrontational, or if you're going to show favorites, then you shouldn't do it. It's not fair to the kids. Their life is going to become more dysfunctional later. You have to be the one who is objective and sensitive. Before you get married, you better figure that out.

Know that you can love your stepkids.

Get in touch with your feelings and see if you can love the kids as your own. Put aside that feeling that I'd rather be with my own kids than with you. It's not enough to love the woman or the man; it's just not. And it won't work. Most people fall in love and think, "Oh, well, I'll love the kids or I'll learn to love them." It's going to bite you back in the butt. Your spouse will turn on you, because hopefully, although not in the case of my mom, the mom or dad is going to try to defend their kids once in a while.

Get help for your problems.

My stepdad came into the Chicano version of a Mexican-American family. He left a whole family behind. He came here, had problems with the language, had problems fitting in. And I feel bad still when I think about everything that happened to this man. But I was the child; I wasn't the adult. So I think it just really could have worked, you know, maybe if my mom and him had tried to work it out with some sort of counseling, or if he would have gone to AA to try to stop drinking. I don't think he ever really tried to stop drinking.

Have regular communication as a family.

Maybe assign a weekly rap session with the family. A lot of people don't want to go to therapy. They are afraid of what it means, that they will get labeled. At the very least, maybe you can look at books to help you have family discussions. How you are feeling today? Is one of the kids feeling jealous or left out? Is one of the children getting served more food than the others? These are things that happen. Communication between the stepdad, biological parent, and the kid is important. If my stepdad could have talked about why he drank, maybe as a family we could have figured out a way to help. It would have made me as a child feel more comfortable at home. I would have grown up less anxious and depressed.

Do things with your kids.

Do activities with your stepkids, whether it's sports or other things. Put it on the kid—what does the kid want to do? Not what does the adult want, but what does the kid want? Do one-on-one things with them. I remember that my stepdad and I fixed houses together sometimes. We'd be outside, sawing wood, and I'd hold the wood, or I'd hold the thing that you do to mark the wood, or whatever I could to help. And that was nice. Those are the only good memories I have of my stepdad.

Sebastian's Advice for Parents

Leave a bad relationship.

Have the courage to leave a bad relationship. I know that everyone wants to love and be loved, but it's not worth the pain that you will put your child through. Don't be selfish, because the kids pay for it. You're the parent. Try really hard to make it work, but if it doesn't, let it go. Just leave. Do not subject your children to violence, drinking, and abuse. It will affect them all their lives, as it has with my brothers and sisters. You had these children. The children did not have any say. Make it easier on them. It's a lot better being a little poor living on food stamps than having a little bit of extra cash but subjecting your children to chaos and violence.

Watch for signs and take action.

Statistics show that many stepfathers and stepmoms have issues with their stepchildren. Are there signs that things are brewing? Are there signs of aggression? Are the stepchildren being picked on too much? Are they having too many chores to do? Are they being spanked too much? Is there a lot of hollering going on? Don't ignore the cues. Remember that children cannot defend themselves. Talk with the stepparent and take action.

Talk with children about their feelings.

Ask—"What's going on? How are you feeling about things" And really talk it over with the child. Really bring problems out into the open. Go to counseling if you need to. There will always be problems. There will be some kind of exchange between the stepparent and child. Be aware and when you see things, address them by talking with the kids.

Sebastian's Advice for Stepchildren

Find an adult to talk with.

I went to Catholic school from first to fourth grade. In the second grade a nun named Sister Lillian took an interest in me. She was a white woman with short gray hair and glasses. It must have been apparent in first grade that I had problems because I was in counseling. She was really nice to me, really took an interest in me, gave me a lot of attention, and took me shopping. Sometimes she'd bring boxes of food to the house. When I fought with kids, instead of saying, "You're a bad kid," she gave me love. That's what kids need. I went into counseling because of her. I saw her a few years ago. I went to tell her that I was alive and wasn't in prison and that I had gone to college. I wanted her to know.

Don't keep your feelings inside.

If something's bothering you and you're feeling kind of sad and hurting and it's in your heart, you should really talk about it. Make it known. First try and talk with your biological parent. If your parent does nothing, find someone else to talk with. Try your aunt or your grandma, your sister, or a nun. Just talk about it. Do not let it go. Opening up and confiding in somebody is the most important thing. Don't keep secrets.

Know that it's not your fault.

Don't blame yourself. Divorce is a parent thing. You kind of think it's your fault. You think you brought it on yourself. This does some kind of negativity to you. Try to get it out of you, so that you don't have that issue. It will affect your self-esteem later in life.

You can survive.

Life is a journey. So far I have used my experience as power. Despite many attempts to keep me down, I am still here. I know there is a reason why I am still alive. So forgive your parents and stepparents, and then move on. Use your experience as strength.

■■■■■■■■■■■■■■■■■■■■■■■■■■■■■■■■■■

Julie

Julie is thirty-one years old. Her parents divorced when she was a year and a half. Her mother remarried soon after and recently divorced. Her father lived with his girlfriend, who is now his wife, for most of Julie's life. She has a stepbrother, stepsister, and a half-brother. Julie is a writer.

Julie's Story

I became a stepchild at age one and a half. I was too young to understand anything. I spent most of my life with my father, his girlfriend Linda, and her son, who was a year and a half younger. When I was very young, I spent days with my dad, who was unemployed, and nights with my mom. As I got older, I spent alternating weeks with each parent. Then when I was six, my mom moved to New York City and I stayed with my dad in Los Angeles, visiting my mom on holidays and during the summer. In second grade I lived in NYC for the full year and visited my dad. But the next year I moved back to LA because my dad missed me, and I missed LA too.

My dad's household was very communal. He had roommates and people always stopped by. I felt like I had a lot of aunts and uncles. But he was very strict. I remember being afraid of my dad and wanting to please him by doing well in school and not getting into trouble.

My mom's house was different in that my stepdad was boss, and I remember being a little scared of him. There were times when he would tell me to do things and I would say, "You're not my dad." He was lenient in some ways, especially when his daughter, who was a year and a half older than I, stayed with us. He would say, "Do you want to go to school or go see *Superman*?" That freaked me out because I never missed school, even when I was sick.

I guess I always considered LA my home because I had so many friends who lived on my street and my grandma lived next door to my house. I would spend every Friday night with her, and she would treat me like a princess.

Mom and Dad

My dad and I are alike. I take after him in that I work hard, expect a lot of myself, and I am practical and good to people. I still like to please him with my job, my house, my friends, the college I select. I know he is proud of me. We share the same sense of humor. The only thing is I have always liked to argue with him for some reason. Sometimes he is short-tempered and we bicker, but while I think it's funny, he takes it seriously. I know he gave me everything. He even sacrificed his relationship with my stepmom Linda for me because he always put me first or equal, and I know she would have liked more attention. When we children moved out, they became closer and more intimate, and I liked seeing that.

I love my mom too. We are more like friends now because I didn't have the typical relationship with her. I didn't grow up in her house. I'm sort of glad I didn't because she's a real "girlie" girl. She likes to dye her eyebrows and hair, look fashionable, and get her nails done. I was a tomboy and a late bloomer. She was always critical of me when she saw me. She'd say, "Your tummy is sticking out" or "Do something with your hair." My dad, on the other hand, didn't care what I looked like as long as I was a good person and did well in school. I think that gave me strength of character that living with my mom wouldn't have. She is self-absorbed and my dad is community-minded. It's funny because while most moms pry in the daughter's business, my mom tells me more about herself and rarely asks me about myself. It's okay though because I've learned to accept her and love other parts of her, like her love of theater. Now we go out to dinner, get our nails done, and have fun like friends. I know I can count on her.

Stepparents

When I was growing up, my dad was in charge of me and my stepmom was in charge of her son. That was how the discipline worked. She never really disciplined me, and she would get upset if my dad yelled at her son. One big thing we clashed about was my use of the telephone. I loved talking to my friends on the phone, and I tied up the line for hours. This was back in the day when we only had one line. Finally my dad got me my own line. But my stepmom liked to talk on the phone, and she would get really mad when I stayed on the line. My dad didn't care so it always came down to my stepmom being mad at me. I didn't care because I thought my calls were very important and necessary. When her son got old enough and started talking on the phone, she got him his own line when he asked for it. She didn't try to understand me when I was going through the same thing.

We also clashed because I thought she gave her son special treatment. Her son and I went to the same school where she taught, and sometimes she gave us rides with her to school. Other times we took the bus. Whenever her son asked for a ride, we would get it. But I could never ask. That bugged me. It was the same with rides home from school. I overcame these differences because I knew my dad favored me and my stepmom favored her son. I knew my life was pretty good, and deep down I was pretty happy. I could tell that my dad loved me to death, so I didn't feel powerless. And I think that's why these things didn't upset me. Plus I had a mom who called me and visited me and I knew she loved me. My stepbrother didn't have a dad after about age seven, so I felt lucky, and I guess I didn't mind sharing my dad. Sometimes when my stepmom and I clashed, I would hurt her feelings. She was very sensitive, but my dad would help us work it out. I would end up apologizing, saying I would try not to do such and such again.

One other thing, and this is funnier than a real clash— is that I was/am pretty chipper in the morning and my stepma and stepbro aren't. So my stepma would always make fun of me and ask me not to talk or be happy so early in the morning. I sort of felt bad that she was putting me down, but then sometimes she would joke about it to other people, and then I knew she was only making fun of me. And over the years, I realized lots of other people aren't morning people either, and she's not alone in thinking my morning "chipperness" can be annoying.

My dad and stepma kept separate food shelves until I was in junior high. I didn't think it was weird. My friends did. But my stepma liked healthy foods and my dad didn't. Of course, we could eat off the other shelves. It wasn't that strict. But I guess I understood it because it was what my dad wanted. He's sort of anal and liked order. And I accepted his way. I think he may be a little obsessive about keeping things in order, but I shared his theory of "mine and yours." I definitely grew up thinking this is yours, and that is mine. I don't like to share.

I really respect my stepmom for a lot of things. She believes in natural, healthy cooking and natural healing.

She turned me on to a great natural healer I love. My stepmom is very caring when I'm sick and offers great natural remedies. Also, she thinks I'm great and is always supporting and encouraging me. She makes me feel good about myself, not in a fake way, but a realistic one. For example, I recently experienced my first heartbreak—at twenty-nine. And her reaction was, "Great, Julie. You're finally feeling what everyone else feels. You were always so hard on people for being emotional about breakups. He really broke through to you." This made me look at my heartbreak as a growth experience. "And besides," she would say, "he wasn't good for you. It was just practice for the real one." And I love that my dad and her have stayed together for over twenty-five years and are happy. They are good for each other and that makes me happy. After my stepbro and I moved out, they were like newly-weds. And they did finally get married a year ago. My dad said he married to set a good example for my brother and me.

My relationship with my stepdad until he died in August 2003 was great. He was generous, supportive, loving, fun, funny, down-to-earth and really good to people. I always got excited to be with him and also nervous because I wanted him to like me. Whenever he was around, I was super aware of him. I tried to make him laugh or talk about things that would interest him. I knew that my mom really loved him, and she was always trying to please him, and so I think I tried too.

I do remember one big thing that might help explain what I mean about being nervous around him. My stepdad was very affectionate and he would always want to kiss me hello and goodbye and goodnight. And I remember being uncomfortable because my dad and stepmom didn't kiss me much. But my stepdad kissed his daughter and son a lot. That was his style of parenting. But I wasn't used to it so I would make a big production, like make him dip me and be dramatic. And one day my mom told me that he didn't like that and I had to stop. And I did. That is an example of how I monitored my behavior.

I knew that my stepdad adored his daughter. And so to make her like me, and probably to make him like me too, I let her cut my hair, dress me, and boss me around. When you first meet someone, you are shy and unsure how to act. A lot of times I was just quiet or didn't act like I would around other people. On the other hand, I knew my dad loved me unconditionally and I could do anything and he would still love me. I knew he would usually stand up for me against my stepmom, so even though I tried to get my stepmom to like me, I didn't worry about her so much. On the flip side, I knew my stepdad had a lot of influence over my mom, and so I wasn't sure she would take my side if I did something to irritate or go against him. She wanted us to get along. We did anyway, but I also felt pressure to make him like me. This was as much my own young person's insecurity as it was reality. I knew he loved me unconditionally. It was just harder for me to be as sure about it.

Over all I wanted to make my mom happy, and I knew making my stepdad happy would make her happy. She did leave California and me to go to New York City when I was six to be with him, so I knew that he was obviously important to her, and maybe deep down inside I thought he was more important to her than me, even though I knew she did love me.

In general, I really didn't rock the boat with either stepparent. I was a good kid. I didn't intentionally want to annoy or disappoint them because I knew my mom and dad really loved and cared about them. I am really flexible because I want everyone to be happy. I probably let my stepdad and stepsis make decisions and didn't consider what I wanted because I thought I would be happy with whatever they wanted. And usually I was happy being flexible. I probably didn't assert myself too much, in the name of keeping peace. But I did that with my friends also, not just with my stepdad and stepsis.

My mom and stepdad separated six years ago, after being together for twenty-five years. She was not speaking to him when he died, but my relationship with him was still strong. He let me know in many ways that he still loved me and was there for me by visiting me, checking up on me, writing and calling when I was having problems, and sending me airplane tickets to visit him and the rest of the family whenever I wanted. He always let me know how much he loved me.

I miss him terribly. I know it was very hard on my mom that he died when they were on bad terms. She talks about it with me a lot and has sought professional help. It's difficult too because while I am empathetic with her pain, I was also very close to him before he died and knew his side of the story, which was different from my mom's. Toward the end of my stepdad's life, my siblings and I were stuck in the middle of our parents' separation.

What I choose to focus on, however, is what an important, influential, and inspiring person my stepdad was, and how I can live up to his greatness in deed and in spirit. He was always so supportive and encouraging of everything I did. He used to brag that I'd be the first female President of the U.S.A. I want to continue to make him proud of me.

Siblings

My relationships with stepsiblings are basically good. My stepsister and I are friendly. I look up to her because she has great style and a nice family—she has a husband

and nine-year-old son. I used to like to bug her but as I grew older, I liked to copy her style of dress and just hang around her and do whatever she did. I let her cut my hair any way she wanted because I wanted to make her happy, and I wanted her to like me. Today I like hanging out with her because she's hip and has cool friends and we like to do similar things like watch movies and eat brunch.

My stepbrother is a great guy. We are good friends. He was always quiet, and I was always active. I had my own friends, but sometimes our friends would all hang out together. We never really had a bad time. We always got along, and I was glad he was in the house. We had a lot of fun on vacations. If anything, I always thought he thought I was too happy and perky. But now he tells me I'm funny and he looks up to me.

I also have a twenty-one-year-old half-brother my mom and stepdad had when I was ten. He was always like my little son that I took care of. I just wanted to do everything for him. I was and still am a pushover. I try to set a good example. I love him so much. It's different from my two other sibling relationships because I feel like a wise guardian to him. I think we all try to help him, so we might be enabling him, but I guess that's what happens when you're the youngest.

Grandparents

My grandma on my dad's side and I are real close. I used to sleep at her house every Friday night, and now I'm her favorite. She takes me shopping and we go out to lunch. She likes girls. She has two grandsons but she basically ignores them, which makes them and their parents mad. I don't know if it's because she likes girls or because I'm friendlier. I have a stepgrandpa, my stepdad's dad, whom I'm close with. He's black because my stepdad is black. It's funny because we hang out a lot when he visits, which is often. He tells everyone I'm his granddaughter, and I know they look puzzled. He's so funny, and he loves me a lot. I hang out with him when he visits more than his real granddaughter does. I knew my mom's mom when I was little and I slept at her house once in a while. We went to McDonald's and then the 5 & 10 store so I could get a gift. I didn't know my dad's dad or mom's dad, so having a stepgrandpa was nice for me. I knew my stepmom's parents but not very well. I would visit them with her and her son, and they were always nice.

Today

My experience as a stepchild has made me see that all people are different, and I have learned not to judge people but rather to accept them. Maybe I wouldn't have chosen to be my stepsister or stepbrother's friend, but they were in my life. They are not like me, not like a real brother or sister might be because we have different parents, but still I had to live with them. It made me accepting of differences. I learned to be easy-going because there were always a lot of different agendas going on. I think it made me sweeter and nicer and able to get along with different types of people. I know it taught me to go with the flow.

One thing I also notice about myself is that I'm flexible, almost too flexible, and I always want to please everyone and make sure everyone's happy. I don't like confrontation. I don't rock the boat. Maybe it's because I think if I do, people won't like me and they'll abandon me. Maybe a good effect is that I am always optimistic. I focus on the positive. This has helped me get along with co-workers. But it also makes me sort of wimpy, easily taken advantage of and manipulated. I have a good sense of self but not an overpoweringly strong one. I tend to have friends who dominate me. As I've gotten older, I've learned to put my foot down and forge my own path, but I think having lots of parents and step/half-siblings made me really eager to please and to be liked by everyone.

My concept of family is love. I had a lot of love. I think I have a different view of marriage than a lot of my friends because they think marriage is forever. I think it's okay to marry someone because you love them and then if years go by and people change and you want to separate, that's okay. It is heartbreaking. But my parents both went on to meet two wonderful people they stayed with and loved for twenty-five years. My dad is still with my stepmom. It's better that my parents split up to be happy with someone else than to stay miserable with each other. And I got great new brothers and sisters from the new marriages. I also learned that my parents are human like everyone else, and they can fall in and out of love. My mom can break hearts, and my dad can get his heart broken. Life ain't easy.

I think all my parents have always known me pretty well. I tell them pretty much everything, and they've always let me express myself and be who I wanted. They never told me who to be, and I never had to hide anything from them. However, I think that now that I'm thirty-one, I'm really getting in touch with some sadness I had locked inside from my childhood, and I'm learning how to express my feelings. I feel like I have a lot of work to do on myself, but I'm old enough to do that sort of work by myself. I think working on myself will be a lifelong process.

Julie's Advice for Stepparents

Don't become the parent.

Don't try to be your stepkid's parents if they already have parents. Be more like a friend and win the kid over by being fun and supportive. The kid is going to put up a fight at first, but it will be pretty easy to win them over if you're not too pushy or authoritative. As an adult friend, you're allowed to say, "That's too much candy; you'll get sick." But you have to slowly gain their trust so that you can really start disciplining and giving them guidance. It also matters what age you enter their lives and, as I said before, whether they have real parents. I think age matters because my stepparents entered my life before I was a year old and so I don't remember what life was like without them or what life was like when my real parents were together. I don't know anything different. That is good because I think if I had been older, I might have resisted friendship, love, and discipline from my stepparents.

My mom tried to parent my stepfather's kid from his previous marriage, and there was terrible fighting between the two women and between my stepdad and mom. Six years ago when my mom and stepdad separated, he said part of the reason, actually the most important reason, was because he didn't like how my mom treated his daughter. In my eyes, it wasn't how she treated her—like abuse or anything—but rather that she tried to raise her as she would her own kid. She tried to get her to have a budget and not buy expensive things, but this was how my stepdad chose to raise her and I think if my mom felt like being with my stepdad, she should have left his child alone. But she couldn't. My stepsister had a mom (who didn't like my mom by the way), so she wasn't looking for a mom. My stepsister's mom liked her to spend my stepdad's money, and he liked it. So who was my mom to say no? My stepsister probably wanted a friend in my mom, and my mom tried to be her mom.

Take the lead from the parent.

My parents welcomed and supported parental help from my stepparents and I saw that. If my dad had rejected my stepmom's attempts to discipline me, I might have followed his lead and rejected her attempts as well. My stepparents were additions and back-up.

Get to know the kid.

Just watch, listen, and observe as with any new relationship. Be open. Be guided by love and acceptance and don't think that this person (the kid) has to like you or listen to you. Just try to get to know the kid.

Julie's Advice for Parents

Stay focused on creating a loving environment.

Parents should focus on loving their kids and new wife/husband. They can't worry too much if everyone will get along. The kid will see that you love this new person and that you still love them. They will need time, but they will learn to accept the situation.

Try to stay on good terms with the other parent.

It also helps the kid if the real parents are still talking and on good terms and that one is not talking badly about the other behind the other's back. My mom and stepdad would stay over at my dad and stepmom's house for a few nights. They ultimately did it for me and because they are all smart and basically good people. They were all happy with the new people in their lives so no one was single and bitter. I think my dad was heartbroken for two years and then got over my mom.

Let the children be themselves.

Allow the children to be themselves; don't pressure your child to love the stepparent. Let them know they can do no wrong when it comes to how they feel. Make sure they know they are important and loved unconditionally. If my mom had shown more backbone in dealing with my stepdad, I would have felt like I had more control in my relationship with him. As it was, I knew my mom was pressuring me to get along with him, even though I did anyway. There was pressure to act certain ways that made me uncomfortable. My mom's life with my stepdad was all about him, and I felt tension and pressure. This was tension that I didn't feel at my dad's house because he put me first and I knew it.

I think this advice pertains to both parents and stepparents but mainly the parent, because the parent is the one the kid looks to as a role model first. The parent sets the pace, and I think my mom set it up so I was uneasy around my stepdad at times.

Julie's Advice for Stepchildren

Stepchildren need to understand that sometimes mommy and daddy are not happy together and want to be with someone else. That's hard for kids to understand but maybe easier for teens. They need to see that more parents means more presents, more love, more opportunities to do things. It's a good lesson in tolerance and accepting people into your life

■■■■■■■■■■■■■■■■■■■■■■■■■■■■■■■

Sarah

Sarah is twenty-six years old and lives with her boy-friend of three years. Her father and stepmother got to-gether when she was four years old, marrying two or three years later. Sarah inherited a stepsister, and later two half-sisters were born. Her mother never remarried. Sarah is a financial analyst.

Sarah's Story

I was four when Mary and her daughter moved in with my father, and I officially became a stepchild two or three years later when they got married. But I feel I became a stepchild when I was four. Initially my parents did their best to try to explain to me what was happening. They always thought it was much harder on me than it really was. It was okay that things were going to change, that there would be two houses. I remember feeling much more okay than I was expected to feel. People would ask, "How do you keep track of where you're supposed to be? Don't you have this very complicated life at home?" I'd say, "No, it's very simple. I live with my mom this week and next week I live with my dad." I remember being in a playgroup and telling my teachers it wasn't a big deal.

When my dad and stepmom moved in together, there was a shift of attention to my stepmom. I felt that my time with my dad was reduced dramatically. For example, we went camping sometime pretty early on in their relation-ship, and I had to stay in a different tent from my dad. That really scared me, and I didn't like it. From the very beginning, there were issues over the role of my stepmom, and all the rules changed. The fact was that she was not my mom, but she had to have some sort of control, some sort of authority. I remember being really resentful. Before Mary, things had been very clear. I was at my mom's house, I was at my dad's house, this was my mom, and this was my dad. Rules with Mary were never clear.

After my dad got married, almost immediately the court decision came down that I would spend three weeks with him and one with my mom, and my mom would have me every other weekend. I was told that the court favored him because he had a family. Suddenly there was this more complicated schedule that I had to understand, and I didn't think my stepmom had the right attitude about it. She seemed to think, "Well, isn't this great? We're going to be more of a family together." And I was thinking, "We're not a family, and I don't want this." I remember that my mom was crushed. Then when I was seven, my dad and stepmom moved to the suburbs and my mom got custody. I spent the weekdays with my mom and three weekends a month with my dad. Summer was split down the middle. That is how it stayed until I graduated from high school.

My Dad

I loved the year when it was just my dad and I, and I always look back with nostalgia on that time. He had his guitar and he would sing me to sleep every night. He wrote two songs for me, one about the afternoon that I was born and another one about seeing the world through the eyes of a little girl. There were other songs, and we would go to hootenannies and protests. When I was little, all these people would come over to the house to sing and talk. Politics was always really important. But after he and Mary were married, his attitude towards everything really changed. I felt my dad should have asked me if it was okay to marry her, because he and I had been a team.

I was always daddy's little girl. I adored him, and I knew I was his favorite. I wanted to spend as much time as possible with him and learn everything he could teach me. He encouraged me to never take what I was told at face value, to question everything, and to develop my own beliefs through questioning until I felt I really understood thoroughly. This encouragement, along with other factors, helped foster in me a strong sense of independence and a fierce stubbornness, qualities he later came to resent. They didn't fit in with the suburban family life he settled into. I have felt especially betrayed that he came to resent those very qualities that he had encouraged in me.

My relationship with him was different from the relationship he had with his other daughters, and not only because he saw me less frequently. I always felt like I knew more about him because I knew him before he was this person in the suburbs. It was always clear to me that I was a favorite, but he couldn't really show off his feelings for me because it made everybody else jealous. I also knew that I didn't fit in because I had this other life and this other world. After they moved, the drive was our time alone. We'd just talk. We would get chocolate and hamburgers because Mary didn't allow anything like that in the house. I felt like this was special time I had with him that he didn't have with the other kids.

Every girl has a point where she realizes that her dad is not perfect. I think I always suspected he wasn't, but it was sort of a big blow to discover the truth. I faced up to the fact that my dad hid behind my stepmom. When my stepmom would tell me that my mom was a liar, he didn't stop her. I was always mad at my stepmom and never really mad at him, and I think that worked for him. He let that happen. It's strange looking back and seeing that for most of my childhood, I believed that he could do no wrong. I once told him, in all seriousness, that I wanted to learn from him everything he could teach me about having a healthy marriage. That seems so blind now. I would blame everything that was wrong with the situation at his house on my stepmom, and even now it's hard for me to remember that he did anything wrong.

He would always say that he wanted me to fit into his family seamlessly and to have this good relationship with my sisters. He always had this family thing. And at one point I got really mad and said, "No, I need to have a relationship with you, and then if that can actually get worked out, then I'll have a relationship with them." I wanted him to relate to me independently of them. I'm not part of that family. Things didn't work out with my mom. He met Mary, had a kid with her, he married her, had another kid with her. He chose that. That's his life. That's separate. He got religion and moved to the suburbs. I was his daughter before that. He was my dad before that.

My Mom

I wasn't as close to my mom as I was to my dad, but I was close. She also taught me to be independent and to think for myself, and she still encourages that today. I was my mom's only child, so I got a lot of attention from her.

I remember that she would tell me never to grow up, just stay little, and yet she was always encouraging about my education and my desire to grow. When I was a child, every Tuesday I got to be the boss and decide what we were going to do. She didn't work on Tuesdays, and I stayed home from school. This was our day. We would make things all the time. There was always a new art project. We would make structures or play with cardboard and paper. I had toys and games that make kids smarter. My mom had this attitude of wanting me to figure things out for myself. She was definitely training me to grow up and study mathematics. Education was always the most important thing at my mom's house, and most of the values I have about education and community came from her.

I haven't always had the easiest relationship with her. She knew that I was hearing propaganda about her from my dad, and she thought I believed it. That made it hard for us to connect sometimes. She was defensive sometimes. I always felt that my mom would always support me, but she wasn't always the person I would go to for emotional support.

She had at least two serious relationships, and I knew that they had to be really serious because she introduced them to me. I understood that she was trying to protect me. I think my mom always assumed that I was going to hate her boyfriends. The rules were really clear with her boyfriends. She was my mom and they had no parental rights. They couldn't tell me what to do. I was not responsible to them. I liked that because I was always protective of the fact that I had two parents. I had two last names. Nobody else should try to pretend to be my dad, or pretend that my dad didn't exist.

The Stepmom

I met my stepmom Mary the day we were going to the Renaissance Fair. She had long, straight black hair and I was sure she was a witch. I remember being scared of her from the beginning. I never really felt that she loved me. I didn't understand her attitude toward the world. It seemed foreign, which makes a lot of sense now that I'm grown up and have a perspective on it. What was important in her house, like how we looked and how we dressed, just never seemed right to me.

My stepmom would do things like put bows in my hair. I would show them to my mom, and she would hate them. One of the highest ideals in the community where my mom and dad lived before he moved away was to have kids who could be anyone. It didn't matter if you were a boy or a girl, you could do whatever you wanted. Girls didn't have to wear dresses or put bows in their hair, but I really liked dresses and things like that.

I didn't feel that I had the right defenses against my stepmom, and I couldn't talk to my dad about it. There were these weird rules about what I was supposed to think towards her. I was supposed to learn to respect her or something like that. It was really awful, and I didn't feel like I could say anything. I remember her driving me home from school and telling me that my mom was an awful liar. She did that kind of thing every day, and it was really horrible. I didn't feel safe with her. I really wanted her to go away.

She wanted to please my dad and would make maternal gestures towards me when he was around. I noticed that her gestures were disingenuous, so I would reject them. Anytime she was nice to me, I resented her more for trying to replace my mom. When she was mean towards me, I resented her more because I felt that proved she was really mean at heart. Anytime she acted towards me with indifference, I resented her more for being indifferent. I blamed her like this for years. She was in a no-win situation. Later I realized that she'd been the focus of my hatred, and that a lot of it should have been directed at my dad, and some of it just wasn't anybody's fault.

Life at Dad's House

My dad's house focused on religion; this was the one

thing that he knew that he could offer that my mom couldn't. And yet everything was always disorganized at his house, and I didn't really have my own space. They had taken it away because I didn't live there all the time. I was encouraged not to do my homework because they said that family time was more important. I hated that because there were times when I needed to figure out a math series or write a paper. I felt that I had to become a different person when I lived there.

There was always pressure to make friends, and they would arrange for me to hang out with their children's friends, which of course was the worst thing they could have done. My dad thought that if I made friends, then I would want to stay there. At my mom's house, it was hard to make friends because I couldn't play with people on the weekends and so I'd miss out on things.

I remember my dad and stepmom telling me that they really wanted me to move there, and for a while I thought that was what I wanted. They said that when I was eleven, I'd be old enough to decide for myself and the court would take me seriously. I remember turning eleven and realizing that I really didn't want that at all, and I had to tell my dad. He was really sad. But I didn't feel like I fit in at his house, and I didn't like my stepmom. I never, ever, ever liked her. When I was fifteen, I said I was fed up with the back-and-forth arrangement and that I wanted to stay with my mom. My mom's house was my home. But it's weird, because there was so much stuff going on that I almost felt as though I didn't have a home.

Siblings

My dad always insisted that I should live with him because he had a family and because interacting with sisters was going to make me a better person. I resented that argument. He was saying that because I was not living with him and didn't have a family, I was going to grow up to be a bad person or an incomplete person. So that made my relationships with his daughters hard because they weren't just people, but symbols of being a better person.

My stepsister Sandra was my age, two months older, which is a big deal when you're four years old. She had long, blonde hair. I was so jealous of her because I was never allowed to grow my hair long. I remember that it was a little weird because I had to share my toys with her, and there was definitely pressure for me to like her. I didn't really like sharing, and I have never liked feeling pressured to like someone. I did not want to think of her as a sister. I did not want to think of her as anything other than a stepsister. I ended up getting her hand-me-downs, which also really bothered me. And yet I don't remember really disliking Sandra, and later we became pretty good friends.

I had just turned six when my half-sister Sally was born. My dad and stepmother got married shortly after that. I really liked her. I knew my mom wasn't going to like it, but I remember clearly thinking that everybody was going to love the new baby and that I was going to pay attention to her when nobody else would. I would wake up with her at four in the morning before my dad and Mary would wake up, and we would go upstairs and play until her mom woke up. I thought she was going to be just like me, and I really liked her a lot.

My half-sister Sabrina was born two years later. I never connected to her, mostly because I didn't see her much. She was also my stepmom's favorite. She's clearly Mary's daughter.

Grandparents

I always considered my dad's parents to be exceptionally special people. They lived on the East Coast, so I only saw them about once a year, but that was frequent enough. I would visit them sometimes with my dad, other times by myself. His other daughters never came along.

I always believed they thought I was exceptional. We never really talked about family issues. To me they were just grandparents, two special people who lived far away but loved me. Visiting them was always a treat, and often their home was a place where I could be independent from my dad's family and my parents' fighting.

On my mom's side, I only had a grandfather. He lived a lot closer and has always been a part of my life, even when he wasn't on speaking terms with my mom. Like my mom, he has always been incredibly supportive. He's encouraged my education and interests, and I deeply respect him.

As I got older, he became an even stronger support, external from my parent's conflicts. As with my dad's parents, we never really talked about family issues. He is a family member I can trust and respect. I depend on him for that small piece of my family that is supportive and free from conflict.

Now

This stepchild experience has affected me in many ways. I developed the skill of adaptability. To fit in, I had to adapt in every way, all the time, to something different. When I went to visit Russia as a high-school exchange student, all the other students had so much more trouble adjusting. When I went to college, the same sort of thing. When I was younger and went away to camp, everybody else would miss his or her mom and dad. I was used to not being with them. There were always times when I was away from one or the other parent. Being away from both was just the same.

The biggest detriment I have from the experience is that it's really hampered my ability to trust. My parents saw the same events differently. They were always telling different stories about the same things. I was never really able to trust my parents, and so today I have a hard time trusting any situation.

I developed a sense of independence. I grew up early, which I think can sometimes be a problem. I think a lot of people when they're younger just sort of follow their parents' philosophy, just go along with it. But because my parents didn't agree on anything, I had to stop and think about things all the way through and develop my own opinions.

Being my dad's favorite and my mom's only child was really good for my ego, maybe a little bit too good. Sometimes I get accused of being arrogant. Sometimes I think I'm just misread. I continually question my social skills and I am introverted. Sometimes I think that because I had to keep so much internalized for so long, I developed a bad habit of internalizing the really awful things.

I was a senior in high school before I figured out that I wanted to have kids and that I could. I really don't want to get divorced, and I can't imagine making the same mistakes my parents did. They didn't seem to think through having a kid together and the long-term commitment that meant. In the high-school exchange program, when I lived with a Russian family, I remember sitting in their house and thinking that I had never really felt like I had a family. It was always just me and my mom, or me and my dad and his family. My mom and I didn't seem complete enough to really be a family; we were missing things. My dad had his family. But sitting in that Russian living room on the other side of the world, in a country that used to be America's enemy, I felt so included and so welcome. I felt like this was more of a family than anything else I had ever experienced.

Nevertheless, I want my parents to know that I consider the whole experience part of who I am today, and I'm proud of who I am today. I know it made me stronger and more independent.

Sarah's Advice for Stepparents

Establish your authority but don't try to replace the mom.

There are situations where the actual parent isn't around much, but in my situation, there was a stepmom and my mom. I didn't want another mother. I didn't want anything that would dishonor my own mother. I think it would have been good if Mary had talked to me about who she was, explaining that she was my dad's wife, that she was still an adult, and children need to follow the rules of adults. She needed to clearly say, "I don't want to replace your mom, but I do want to have a relationship with you and help you grow up."

I would recommend that a good level of authority for a stepparent is that of any adult who supervises a child, but no more. They should have authority over the immediate situation, but not over lifestyle situations (the same authority an adult has over their kid's friends who come to play).

Allow each child individuality.

I always felt that that my stepmom was jealous of me in a lot of ways. Her children were different from me, and that got translated into jealousy. What should have been recognized is that we were just different from each other. For example, "This is what they are good at and this is what Sarah's good at, and these are problems they have and this is how we should nurture them, and these are problems Sarah has and this is how we should nurture her." Instead, the differences gave us just one more thing we couldn't talk about. It felt like Mary wanted me to stop studying. It was as though she said, "You might be this great student, and this is all really important to your mom, but my children have a family."

Sarah's Advice for Parents

Respect your child's relationship with the other parent.

I think the worse thing my dad did to aggravate an already difficult divorce and custody arrangement was to try to replace my mom with his new wife. I feel that this was so wrong of him. When I was with my mom, I knew that she didn't like my dad, but I also knew that she respected that he was my dad and that he was important to me. She never tried to interfere with my connection to him. Eventually, when I chose to live only with my mom, I felt that my relationship with my dad was safe.

My dad, on the other hand, moved to the edge of the county to force a sole custody situation, and sued in court for a new living arrangement with his new wife as the "sole maternal figure." He wanted my stepmom to become my new mom, and he tried really hard to force that to happen. In his house, I did not feel that my relationship with my mom was safe, and when I learned that he had planned to replace her, I told him I couldn't go to his house ever again. It is wrong to demean a mother to her child.

Remember your original family; don't push too hard.

I felt like my dad had an obligation to me first because I was part of the original family and this was the new one. I felt they wanted to cover that up. By replacing his life with this new family, he was replacing my life and my family, the family I had. He really wanted to drop that old life, and I was a reminder of it. I couldn't accept the fact that he had this new life and he had these new kids, and he and Mary chose to raise their children the way they did. He should not have put pressure on me to accept these people as my full, complete sisters, but to accept them as his other children

I wanted him to acknowledge that it was different with me than it was with the other kids. I have a different mom, and I had a different upbringing up to a certain point. He wanted me to just blend in because that was easier for him, and there was a lot of pressure on me to fit in, which I did not like. One of my dad's biggest mistakes was not to accept me as a different child with a different life. I felt like he and Mary were trying to replace my world and my life, and that was really hard. There was pressure to accept the other kids as my full sisters. Sharing a room with them was part of that; going to school with them was part of that. However, I was always really firm that I had two names, my mom's and dad's. Yes, he was married before, and yes, I had a different mom, and yes, I was Jewish, and yes, they could not take me in public without my talking about these things. Mary hated it. She thought it made them look bad.

Now he's really open about the fact that he has a daughter from a previous marriage, but I think that was really hard for him. He and Mary didn't like to say it in public. It spoiled the image they were trying to create, which then made it harder for me because I knew that I was the one who had spoiled it.

Don't move too far away from the other parent.

I don't think my dad and stepmom should have moved so far away, and whatever reason they had for doing that was not smart. Moving away did not help. I couldn't be involved in extracurricular activities unless I was around on the weekends. And so I started doing more and more things on the weekends at my mom's and spending less time with my dad. Sometimes I'd go to my dad's house for only one weekend night, and I'd leave Sunday morning. Or I'd leave Saturday afternoon. Or I wouldn't go at all, which was sort of a big deal.

Find values that both households share.

I wish that my parents could have agreed on a common parenting philosophy, values they would teach me, and interests they would encourage. I wish that my dad and stepmom had understood that my stepmom's philosophy, values, and interests didn't belong in my life.

There wasn't anything that both parents supported— period. When I was with my dad, the ideals and things that were important to my mom were bad. And from my mom's point of view, suburbia was really bad for children. Mary didn't work outside of the home, and that was bad too. I was becoming more and more aware that I had to be two people, one for my mom and one for my dad. I felt for a long time that I didn't really know who I was.

Don't say bad things about the other parent.

Try not to criticize the other parents.. Sometimes my dad and stepmom would talk to me about my mom. They would call her a liar and say other negative things, and I would then have to defend my mom. I didn't like this.

If you can't control yourself from saying bad things or you can't control your reactions to what you hear about the other parent, then you shouldn't bring the subject up. My mom always asked about what I did at my dad's house, and I knew that she would react badly so I wouldn't want to talk about it. Sometimes my mom would feel that I was hiding things from her. But I wasn't hiding things to hide things; I was just hiding them to not get a bad reaction. But it would have been great if I could have talked about what I did at the other house, and if she'd been able to look at those things without being offended.

I overheard a lot of things that I should not have. My parents were not very careful about what they said to their friends. The adults talked among themselves and everything got back to everybody, and there was no way for me to talk to anyone. I remember being really quiet

Arrange to spend time alone with your child.

I wanted to spend time with my dad. I would go out there to spend time with him, and instead I spent it with other people. He wanted me to spend time with his kids and their friends, and he wanted me to spend time with my stepmom. Sometimes I would go all the way out there and he would be in Atlanta or somewhere far away, and I'd be stuck at the house. It seemed like he wanted me there just so I was away from my mom, and that was really hard

Think through custody issues carefully.

I understand kids who say that a sole custody arrangement would be best, and eventually when I had a little more than two years of high school left, that was the option I chose. But for most of my childhood, separation from either of my parents was something that I flat out opposed. When I eventually chose it, I did so only because the conditions of the joint custody were no longer viable.

I remember very clearly that one of my deepest fears was that some day one of my parents would stop wanting custody of me. As hard as the custody arrangement was, it was very important to me that I be raised by both of my parents. I just wanted it to be easier. It became hard for me to see both parents together because of the hostility. One thing that made it hard was the ever-present possibility that one of them would sue for more time. This thought controlled all our actions with each other. I wanted a stable custody arrangement.

Ask your children what they think.

I feel that my dad and I had a pact. I was there when he asked Mary to move in and when he decided to get married. I should have been part of those decisions even though I was only four. He could have said, "You know, I've met this woman and I really like her a lot and I'd like her to come live with us." And I can't imagine what I would have said. I might have said, "No. I don't like her at all. I think she's a witch." Then we could have talked about that.

My mom had a good way of at least making me believe that I was part of all the decisions, and I don't really know how she did this. I'm sure that the decisions were already made at the time, but I felt that we decided together.

Sarah's Advice for Stepchildren

Find books.

There are books out there that tell kids to ask themselves questions like "How does this make you feel? Do you really want this to happen? How would you want things to be different? What do you imagine?" Find these books. They can help you cope.

Remember—You are loved.

Remember that your parents really do love you. Because they do, you can talk to them. You don't have to accept what's going on. You are part of this family; you exist. You should tell them what you don't like and what you do like and what hurts.

■■■■■■■■■■■■■■■■■■■■■■■■■■■■■■■■■

Kate

Kate is thirty-four years old. She became a stepchild at sixteen when her dad married her stepmother, and then again at seventeen when her mother married her stepfather. Both marriages ended in divorce. Kate has seven siblings and from her father's second marriage a half-brother. She is an actress. She has been married for two years and recently gave birth to her first child, a daughter.

Kate's Story

My parents split up when I was ten, after almost twenty-three years of marriage. It absolutely shattered everyone in my family's world. For six years we all thought and hoped they would reconcile. But it was not to be. My dad married Jennifer, who became my stepmother on my sixteenth birthday. The wedding was in her hometown of Kansas City, and we were not invited. I think that my dad thought, "Everything's going to be fine; just thought it would be easier if you weren't there because—I didn't want to bother you guys." The truth is we probably wouldn't have wanted to go, and it probably would have been very uncomfortable. But still—you know? It was just so weird.

My mom was exactly the opposite. She was like, "Here's Donald, he's going to be your new dad. He's going to move in with us, and you'd better like him," shoving it in our faces. "Come to the wedding and be happy with me." This was when I was seventeen. I remember getting so drunk at that wedding, sitting over in the corner doing shots. She never once said, "Gosh, this must be hard for you." I don't necessarily blame her. I think if she had thought of that, she would not have married, because at her core, she's a mother. That's really her archetypal identity.

I always lived at my mom's house. My mom's house was the house we had grown up in. That was definitely our home. That even felt like our home until she sold it last year. Once my dad moved out, I never went to live with him. At first he had a house in town, where we would visit him and occasionally spend the night, but there were too many of us to have our own rooms. I don't think that it occurred to my dad to make it feel like it was our home. My older brother lived with him during this period, which was strange, like two bachelors, instead of father and son. At that point in his life he was drinking a lot, very depressed, not happy about what he had done and so he didn't feel any impulse to welcome us into his misery, even though he tried and tried to connect and always put on a happy face.

Once he was married, I didn't visit very often. My stepmother wasn't too interested in having relationships with us. It was always very cordial, very surface. She was nice as pie, but it felt more like we were guests in our own father's home. Her hair and her powder-blue eye shadow were always perfect. There was one time, this was later, but it really tells who she is. It was Christmas, a few days after, actually, and we had all gathered at my grandma's for our holiday with Dad. My stepmother was very sick, he told us, which is why she stayed up in the bedroom. Too sick to come down and say hi on Christmas. My sisters went up to see her, to be nice and all, and there she was, sitting up in bed reading, her hair blow-dried, full makeup on her face.

In the Beginning, there was Family

My family is huge. My parents had eight kids, and I was the seventh of the eight, and so by the time I realized what was going on, I was already part of a three-ring circus. But we had a lot of fun, and there was always noise and laughter and chatter and activity. Most of us were all very, very active in sports or arts or clubs or, you know, things. And our parents were always that way too. Both my parents were very involved in the community, president of whatever group they were involved in, whether it was PTA or Direct Relief. They were very visible, very well liked. Mostly, they showed us how to be contributing members of our community. And then of course church. We grew up Catholic, so we had church on Sundays and Sunday school, and that whole thing. And I think that that colored our view of family. I came into being and there was this structure. There was the family and then surrounding it was the community, and at its base was the church. (And it wasn't just my family; I have a huge extended family. I have over fifty first cousins.) My parents and God were about the same in my eyes. You have to understand; my parents never fought. I mean, never. They were, as far as we all knew, a perfect couple, an indestructible institution.

Dad had a corny, corny sense of humor. And he was so dear, really loving and sweet. And at the same time he was a doctor and an Aquarius, so he would check out. He was not always right here. And then also because he was a doctor, he was on call all the time. So he was busy. I mean, we really didn't see him that much. I have very strong memories of him coming home at night and us besieging him, wanting attention and wanting to play with him. And he just wanted to sit and read the paper, which we didn't understand. But at the same time he was also really, really fun, and he was the kind of dad who would take us on ski trips and take us on sailing trips and camping. He really wanted to give us an experience of life outside our little world. He would take us out into nature. I mean, imagine taking eight kids skiing. What a pain! But my parents did it; they did it all the time. They were really great like that. My dad with his crazy ideas and my mom going along with everything, smiling.

My mom was the ultimate full-time mom. That was what she wanted to do with her life. She wasn't a frustrated something; her goal in life was to be a great mom and to become a grandmother. So she was incredibly warm and devoted. I mean, *warm* is really the number-one adjective that comes to mind. And of course, she had too many kids. It was kind of insane. A lot of the time I knew my mom really cared, but she was just kind of very busy, dealing with a whole household. Of course she had help cleaning the house and everything, but imagine ten people's laundry, ten people's meals, cleaning, everything. It was just ridiculous.

My mom got married at twenty-two. She was a virgin. So was my dad, for that matter. Before they were married three months, she was pregnant. And boom, before you know it there were eight mouths calling for mom and dad, and not much room for the man and wife.

Stepmom Jennifer and Dad

My sister June and I met Jennifer, our stepmother, when we visited Dad on New Year's Eve. We were in denial about it, didn't really want to face it. She was of course saccharinely sweet to us. She has this incredibly fake veneer, and I don't really think there's a whole lot behind it. I think she's one of those people whose soul is about this deep. And really I say that with no contempt at all. She was young. She's only probably six or eight years older than my oldest sister. By that time, we were so used to things not going our way. You know what I mean? We just didn't really have any feeling of impact or power in this situation. We were helpless, and we just had to sit back and watch.

Jennifer is a Southern girl from Kansas. She's a plastic surgery nurse, and that's how she and my dad met. On one level, she's bright. To do that kind of work, you have to have some intelligence. She would be really, really sweet as pie to us but ultimately very distant. She was never just real. It was always putting on a very, very happy face. And, at the same time, because she was thirty-seven with no kids of her own, she was used to her own space. And we were used to our own space, but we were also very used to our spaces getting totally encroached upon. So we would come over, and you could just tell that she would just kind of tense up with all the noise and the activity and, well, "Who's using that towel and is it going to get folded again?" You know what I mean? And then pretty soon after they got married, ironically, she ended up getting pregnant. She had specifically told my dad she didn't want kids.

They had a lot, a lot, a lot of fights about money, especially about the money that he would spend on us. Particularly he gave my brother a lot of money and help, because he needed it. She really resented him giving us money. She was so threatened by that. It was just kind of gross.

Stepdad Donald and Mom

My stepdad Donald was another story. His wife had died of cancer. He had fraternal twins, a boy and a girl, and their mother had only died like maybe less than a year before he started dating my mom. His kids were in the same position that we were. They're a few years younger than me. They were really sweet, lovely kids. Donald owned a teddy bear store. There's no harm in that, stuffed animals bring a lot of joy to children, and I certainly had a lot when I was young. But it was really an extension of his personality. On every occasion he would give my mom another teddy bear or stuffed animal. It was like that was his way of expressing affection, to give a grown-up woman teddy bears.

He was okay at first. But then he started to want to hug us hello and good-bye. Prematurely. You know, there wasn't an organic development of our relationship. It was very much pushed upon us, and we were supposed to suddenly like this guy, respect this guy, and want to be involved in his life and have him involved in ours.

It got to the point where, say, Donald would walk into the kitchen, which was the center of our household, of course, big kitchen, and it's busy. It's crazy: the TV's on in the other room, we're cooking, frying pan sizzling, you know. "Oh, good morning, whatever." Or sometimes you'd miss a good morning, and it wasn't totally intentional, but it got to be a thing with him, and he complained to my mom. She said to us, "Well, you have to say good morning to Donald." Or "You have to treat Donald with respect." And our thing to her was, "Mom, he has to earn our respect. He can't just come in here and expect to be this person that we have accepted; we haven't accepted him yet. So we'll try to remember to say good morning, but it's going to be forced."

I loved his kids. We were in the same boat, so we were totally simpatico from day one. They didn't really want to move into our house; they were freaking. And so I instinctually reached out to them. I included them in things because I knew that they thought I was kind of cool because I was a few years older and was with the popular crowd. So it would make them feel good if at lunchtime I would go talk to them and stuff like that.

I'd have to say that Donald was a good person. I'm sure his intentions were good and he wasn't abusive. But he just didn't get it. He just didn't get it. He was the goober to end all goobers. And of course, at that time I'm seventeen; I'm a senior in high school; I drive; I have my own life. I have my boyfriend; I have my cheerleading practice; I'm on the volleyball team; I'm in student government; I'm auditioning for commercials and TV shows. I really don't have room for another person. I was really in no need of any more parenting as far as I was concerned. Donald made my mom choose between him and me, and what did he think she would do? So he moved out.

Siblings; Lots of Them

My siblings include three girls and a boy followed by three girls and a boy. The order is: Abigail, Bernadette, Margaret, John, Ellen, June, me, and David. The first half of the family is very different from the second half. There's about a thirteen-and-a-half year span. The first half of the family were all very innocent. They were like good boys and girls, and they did not hang out with the popular crowd and go out and drink and party. They were good kids. And then the second half of the family, we were all bad kids; we were wild. I don't know if it still would have been that way without the divorce, but it seems to me there was an abrupt change in everyone when it happened. I do know that two of these older sisters were still virgins, and when the split happened, they promptly went out and had sex.

I was always enamored of my older brothers and sisters because they were very sweet to me, took care of us, changed our diapers, read to us. My older sister Abigail would play guitar and sing with us; my sister Bernadette would do theater stuff because she had a wild imagination, and Margaret was a nurse and mommy type. Then they went off to college. I related to them differently than my brother and my other two sisters who were just older than me because I was around the younger ones more. June and I had a lot of fights, typical sibling stuff, and Ellen was this golden child. She just kind of had it all. And I felt really bad for my little brother David, who came to know disappointment so early.

My older brother was totally my hero. John was the oldest one around because the others were in college when the news of the divorce broke. He really took on, as a lot of young men do, a big responsibility to become the man. That was detrimental to him because a sixteen-year-old young man, while he is a young man, is still a boy. Mentally and emotionally, he is still a boy.

Initially the divorce spun us out, but then it spun us back together, and we would have many conversations about the new husband and new wife. We heavily bonded because of it. We consciously saw the devastation, not just in ourselves but also in each other, and made the decision to not take marriage lightly, and not ever take divorce as a way out. It is so, so devastating, not just for the kids, but we found out later on that neither my mom nor dad, had they to do it over, would have done it again.

My half-brother Ron, my dad and Jennifer's son, is great. He's incredibly smart. He's talented intellectually, academically, and athletically. He's a nice, nice boy. He is much more like our dad than his mother. Thank God. We would never "dis" her in front of him. I don't want anyone to feel badly about his or her mother.

Grandparents and the Rest of the Family.

My dad's mother is still alive; she's my last grandma alive. My mom used to drop me off, and I would spend a whole week up there with them in the summertime. They were so sweet. My grandpa and I would play cards for hours, and he would always kind of let me win. But we would play rummy, or cribbage, or euchre, you know, those really great Midwestern card games. And Grandma would teach me how to knit or crochet, or we would maybe make a pie.

And then on the other side, my mom's father died when I was five, so I never really knew him. But my mom's mom and that whole side of the family, all my aunts and uncles and cousins, were very pissed off at my dad. They thought he was the anti-Christ. Seriously. I mean in this whole huge, huge family there had been maybe only one divorce, but it was some second cousin twice removed and nobody even knew him. So divorce was so foreign. And as I said, we were the golden family, so it rocked everyone else, too.

On one side, no one was talking about it, and on the other side, people were talking shit. Well, that's so hard, because as I said, I had worshipped my dad. And while I didn't agree with what he had done, and I was very hurt by what he had done, the moment someone criticized him, I was like, "Hey!"

Scars, but Good Things too

If you take away the foundation of a child's life, then he or she doesn't know where to stand. That's why kids start acting out. Hence, I got very involved with partying. Often I definitely sought the affection of boys.

I think I was at my core a little bit of an insecure person anyway. But the divorce made it worse, because then I had a whole abandonment issue. So I would get involved with people who didn't really want to be involved. Or it wasn't the right time. Or they were emotionally unavailable, kind of like my dad, kind of checked out.

I was totally needy of attention. I think that I've learned how to become an actor who's not needy of attention, but I'm sure that that was a big part of my initial desire to get involved with acting. So yes, the divorce had a profound impact.

In general, I'm very bad with goodbyes. Even just socially, just saying goodbye at a party; I freak out. I hate it. I'm getting better because I've actually come to believe that it's important to say hello and goodbye. Saying goodbye and saying thank you, and ending it, and then knowing that it can come back. I think I have more faith now that life will always give you something else. There's always another corner. But at the time I don't think I really believed that. I want to trust people. Generally. My first impulse is I want to believe them; I want to give them the benefit of the doubt and trust them. But at the same time, only so far. I kind of realized a few years back that I was really keeping people away. I didn't really want to trust them because then they could really hurt me.

I seem incredibly confident. I'm outgoing and friendly, but oftentimes that has been a big mask for a person who absolutely knows she doesn't belong. I've always planned that when I get married, that's it. I'm married for life. I mean, I know most people don't go into a marriage thinking they're going to get divorced. But I do think a lot of people have it in the back of their minds, "Well, if this doesn't work out, I can always leave." And I don't feel that way. It's you and me together, climbing on a ladder. We're not going to back out of this thing. I don't know if I would have had such a strong commitment had my parents' divorce not happened.

One of the really positive things is that I'm super sensitive to children. If I'm in a room with kids and I notice one of them isn't involved, it breaks my heart, and I will immediately go over and start playing with that child. I'm really, really sensitive to kids feeling left out.

I think I'm also really pro-active in keeping the family together. If you asked my family about me, they would say that one of their favorite things about me is that I really make the effort. I show up at the birthday party; I show up at the dinner thing; I drive distances to go see them. I'm kind of like the person who wants everybody to get involved. I think that's kind of my personality anyway, but now I'm sure it's stronger. And then I think also about the whole thing about being real. For example, when I started teaching, I noticed my immediate tendency was to put on a face. And I noticed that kids see right through it. And so, I just thought, "Oh, okay, I don't want to be that adult that I saw when I was twelve, who I knew was bullshitting me. So I'm going to be really real with this kid, and not try to pretend to be anything I'm not."

In the End, there is Still Family

Since the original interviews, I have gotten married, lost my father, and had a baby. These are major events, which also color my responses. But my concept of family remains intact. Family is noise. Family is everything. It's hard to describe it. My husband told me that I couldn't really move away because I couldn't be away from my family. I never said that; he just said that as an observation seeing the way that I am. And sure enough he is right. When Dad was sick, one day my sister and I were in a clinic. We were handling stuff and my dad was taking a nap. Someone said something to us about how they loved the way we were with our father. And we thought, "How else would we be? Of course we're gong to take care of him; of course we would be sweet with him. Are there people who wouldn't do this for their father?" Despite all the craziness that happened, everyone in my family is important to each other.

The most amazing end to their story, by the way, is that when Dad got sick, my mom had already totally forgiven him. There was nothing left but a deep love, a dear friendship. She was able to really be there for him and to take care of him. We were all taking turns and she was right there, without hesitation. At my wedding they sat together, no more stepparents in the picture, and looked as if they'd been together all along. And she was at his side when he died.

Becoming a parent for the first time gives a very different and more understanding perspective on the choices my parents made. What I want them to know is that I have forgiven them for all the mistakes they made. And as a bonus, I have learned from all their mistakes, so they were not made in vain.

I am committed to my marriage—not just staying together, but keeping it alive. It is not an institution but a living organism, which needs constant care and nurturing. We will never stop being a man and woman who are in love, even as we face the challenges of parenting. This is something we have talked about and agreed on. All my married siblings (seven out of nine) are in healthy marriages. I think it is safe to say that their commitments to their relationships have a lot to do with not repeating our parents' mistakes.

My father knows a lot more now than he did when he was alive. Maybe that is the payoff—you trade in your human body for the wisdom you sought all your living days. One thing I really appreciate now is that as a dying man, he didn't air his crap in front of us, even though at the time I wanted him to talk about it more. I wanted to know what he was really thinking and feeling, to share the agony, the discovery, whatever. But he didn't really want to get too deep into it. That was his way of taking care of us. He knew how much we wanted him to stay alive, and so he kept a positive attitude for us. I went to see him in the ICU a week before he died. His lungs were filled with fluid, his body hooked up to machines and tubes and needles. When I asked the ridiculous question—"How are you feeling?" His answer was a cheerful, if barely audible, "Top drawer."

He began this change long before he got sick. His life hadn't really gotten any easier—he was still working full time, Jennifer had left him a few years before, and he was raising a teenage son without much help. But he stopped making his problems our problems. So different from the man who in the years following my parents' breakup would have us over for dinner, drink five vodkas, and then get maudlin telling us how much he loved our mother and how he didn't know how it had all happened. So I guess I'd like to say thank you for taking responsibility for your life and for growing up.

When I look at his life as a whole, and I mean the good, the bad, and the ugly, all his strengths and weaknesses, I am grateful for all of it. I still think I had (have) the best dad I could possibly ask for, and that makes me feel like a lucky girl.

And my mother, I have a great deal of appreciation for all the work it took to raise so many children. I marvel really that she put dinner on the table every night for a large mass of noisy limbs and mouths, and did it because she wanted to. So I want to say thanks for that.

Over time she has been willing to acknowledge her mistakes. She has listened, generously, while I tell her how angry and disappointed I was, and how it continued to affect me as a young adult. She has tried to make up for it, expressed her apology, and given me what she can by way of explanation. It takes a strong, loving person to do this.

So I want to acknowledge her commitment to our relationship, and to her own personal growth.

Eventually, hopefully, we all do grow up. Because it is a lesser strain on one's life to forgive than to resent, I am now able to see my parents as people, not just as my parents. I'm not angry with them for making mistakes anymore, and somehow everything has eased up. There's a freedom in that. So now I can say, "Okay, you're still my dad or you're still my mom, even though you are also a whole human being."

Kate's Advice for Stepparents

Know what you are getting into.

Don't marry a guy with eight kids and then think that they're not going to be involved. As much as I keep saying that my mom is really a mom, my dad was the same kind of a dad. He loved being a dad. His favorite thing was when we were all with him. He loved it. And so my stepmother must have known that about him. It was like, "Dad, doesn't she know that your favorite thing is to have us all over for dinner? And have all the noise and the chaos and the love and the craziness? You love that; how could you marry someone who doesn't?"

Don't move too fast.

I think you have to be really, really gentle with bringing a new person into a kid's life. You have to introduce him or her incredibly gradually, and let the kids feel like they're in control of how close this person's coming. Don't just all go on a weekend together the first time you meet. That's a lot of togetherness. How about just a little dinner? Then how about maybe a week later we'll go to the beach? Kids are not going to tell you how they feel, because they don't know how. But they're going to have feelings. And they'll just go fly their kite or play the piano or do what they're going to do and you won't really know what's going on. If you're the grownup saying, "Okay, we're all going to be happy here," you're just pushing the program. The kid may seem fine, but don't assume that that kid is fine.

Don't take the rejection personally.

You're coming to the party late. Something disruptive happened before you got there, and now you're in a shitstorm. Unless you were the party that caused the breakup (and in that case, DO take it personally), you would be wise to keep your cool and learn how to rise above and deflect the anger that's really intended for the parent. Don't make yourself an easy target by taking the bait.

Respect the child's relationship with the parent.

If you see that the kid is acting out, rather than say, "Let's all go to Magic Mountain together," be wise about it; back off. You might say to the kid and your spouse, "Why don't you two go together? I have lots of things to do. You guys go and have a good day." Look what a rock star you would look like. The kid has a good day and bonds with the parent, and you were generous enough to back off.

Don't think you have to be the parent. You are not!

Of course, this is coming from the perspective of a teenage stepchild...but anyway, remember that there is an important place in a kid's life for a non-parental, adult influence. You can be a wise and compassionate adult by honoring the child's feelings, space, and process. Be real with them; show by example what it looks like to take responsibility for your own journey. Kids have major B.S. detectors, and at the same time, they gravitate toward what's sincere.

Kate's Advice for Parents

Pay special attention to your children.

Even if your divorce was not as devastating as ours, remember that you have taken away the foundation of your child's world. You will need to take extra care to create a new kind of security for them. If I had a son or a daughter, and I had a new boyfriend that I was trying to bring in—God forbid this ever happens to me—I would probably want to make a real concerted effort to spend a lot of time with that kid one on one, so that the kid knew that he or she was still important to me. If I knew that the kid loved to go take walks in the creek and look for tadpoles, I'd really make a big effort to go do that. Or if I knew that this kid really loved moto-cross, I'd take him to the bike park. Make your kids feel like you're not abandoning them, like you're not suddenly so concerned with all your own drama that you've totally forgotten how to be a parent to them.

Deal with the grief, both yours and your children's.

My parents didn't realize that we would grieve. You know, we lost our family and we were grieving. It didn't occur to them that we might need to feel some power in that situation. Grief is such a powerless feeling. I don't think my parents ever said, "Okay, so this is a family problem." It was sort of like "This is our problem; it's not your problem. We love you; you're great." And it never occurred to them to say, "Well, God, wow, this is going to have a huge impact on our kids; they're going to take it on," and children always do.

The family needs to talk about this. You can't just sort of pretend that it's not happening. I think denial is just the worst, worst thing. My advice is for parents to contact a child psychologist or get a book to find out what a three-year-old can process, or a five-year-old. Dovetail your knowledge of your kid with what the experts say and share with your children as much as they can handle. Give the kids permission to feel bad. And a little later help them move towards acceptance.

Both of my parents tried to hide their grief. Their intentions were good. They were trying to protect us. But then what happens is that the kids end up being a little bit shut out. Then they may start acting weird, and then everyone becomes strangers.

What a great experience for kids to see that you can go through something so emotionally devastating, and at the same time still be connected, still get your work done, and eventually get through it and be okay. There's a lot of arrested emotional development in my family because so much was withheld. It was never made clear to us that "Hey, life gets rough and life gets okay, and you just keep going."

Be real and share your feelings so your kids don't feel cut off, and at the same time make sure you are really taking care of yourself and your stuff. And if you need to go to therapy, go. If you need to have time with your friends and cry and cry and cry, do it. Whatever it is that you need to do to handle it, do it. Make sure you do this, so that when you're with your kids and stuff comes up, at least you have processed it somewhat.

Consider the children's opinions.

If you have older kids who are rejecting your choice of new mate, consider for a moment that there is a reason. Sure, they might be taking it out on the new person unfairly, but they might also be clueing you in to something. They know you pretty well; maybe this new person isn't up to snuff. There were people my parents dated that I didn't totally hate, ones I would have been far more open to. Ones I even liked! But the ones that were chosen were not up to standard. Both my parent's second marriages ended, my mom's after only four years. She finally agreed that he was a dud. If she'd listened to us, we could have saved her a lot of trouble!

Kate's Advice for Stepchildren

The divorce is not your fault.

You need to really get clear with the fact that none of this is your fault. Parents need to really make sure that kids are in no way taking on the blame of what happened or the responsibility for making the family work or making things better. It's a totally natural reaction, but unfortunately, our parents are not perfect, and they are making mistakes. It seems so unfair that their bad choices have such an impact on your life. But they are not trying to hurt you.

Comfort your parents, but take care of yourself.

Comfort your parents, but take as much time and care to take care of yourself. That means enjoying friends, being in theater, joining a club—something that is yours, something that you have a stake in.

If I had had the courage, I would have sat with my mom when she was crying. That's not as much shouldering a burden as much as it is being loving, like when you're crying and your dog comes over and knows you're upset. He can't do anything; he just wants to be by you. You can comfort your parents, but don't neglect your own needs.

More than anything, you have an obligation to be a kid. You'll never get to be a kid again. You'll never be fifteen again. Just because this is going on, it doesn't mean that you have to do anything differently. Your obligation is to enjoy your childhood. Be on your volleyball team, take your ballet class—whatever it is you're doing, continue it and enjoy it.

■■■■■■■■■■■■■■■■■■■■■■■■■■■■■■■■■

Sam

Sam is thirty-one years old. His parents divorced when he was two and each remarried before Sam was five. Both marriages ended in divorce, and his father remarried for a third time. His stepfather also remarried. Sam has four siblings: an older brother from his mother and father, a half sister from his mother and stepfather, and two stepbrothers from his father and stepmother. Sam is a high school science teacher.

Sam's Story

My biological parents got a divorce when I was two. I didn't have a lot of emotional development at that point and my memories are sketchy. I do know that by the time I was five, my dad was remarried to Cindy and my mom to Michael. When I was five, my mom and Michael moved from Indiana to Oregon and it was then that the concept of stepparent hit me. It was not explained to me before that. I remember that they entered me into school with my stepfather's name, and that seemed wrong to me. I had a dad; I had a name. They wisely changed their minds and let me keep my name.

Oregon was my home with Mom, Michael, and later with my sister Lois. That was the house I came home to. That is where I spent the night. They were the people who were providing for my needs. I had a role in figuring out what my place was. It was obvious to me that I was an integral part of the decisions.

In Sacramento where I visited with my dad, stepmom,

and stepbrothers, I shared a room with one of my brothers. Even though there was an extra bed there, it never felt like home. It wasn't a place that I got used to because I was only there for two or three weeks every year, and then I would return to my mom and Michael. I was a special visitor.

Two Very Different Households

There was a real big disconnect in terms of parenting styles in the two different households. For example, in Oregon we would try to have dinner together, but there wasn't a specific ritual about it. When the food was ready, we'd all sit down and eat together. Eating dinner at my dad's was very tense. The best way I can describe it is with an example. One time when I was trying to finish a bowl of soup, I was going clang, clang, clang and Cindy my stepmother was very annoyed by that and said, "Why don't you just pick up the bowl and slurp it?" And then she went into the other room. I picked up the bowl and started slurping. She came back and gave me this icy stare. I tried to minimize the number of times that icy stare of doom would come at me.

At my dad's house, there were always chores, and the chores were well-defined kinds of activities. In Oregon, there was stuff that needed to be done and there were chores and different responsibilities, but it wasn't so strict. In Sacramento, it was kind of like you needed to be doing these things every day, like sweeping the kitchen or vacuuming the living room, and checking them off when you did them. These chores were officially assigned to people, and they were rotated. In Oregon, there was an understanding that things needed to be done, but the attitude was "It looks like the kitchen is kind of dirty; can you clean that up?"

Two Fathers

My first memory of Michael, my stepfather, is vivid. I came downstairs one morning and there he was. At that time he was following a guru, and he would often meditate. When he meditated, he sat with his legs crossed and often had a blanket draped over him. I remember coming into my mom's bedroom. My mom wasn't around, but there was a blanket draped over this huge shape on the bed. He was like a point because obviously he was sitting under there and his head was up there. I was thinking, "Whoa, I wonder if I got a present?" I put two and two together and realized that there wasn't a present under there; it was Michael.

I got on with him fairly well. He was very patient and reserved, to both his detriment and to his benefit. He didn't really talk about his feelings that much and didn't show a lot of emotion when he was upset. He wasn't a shouting, screaming type person. He was very solid. If you came in upset, his emotional state was accessible. You could feel pretty much like he was going to listen and that he was going to care about what was going on.

A lot of time Michael stayed home with me. He did the cooking and cleaning or whatever. Michael made wooden toys and sold them in craft fairs for a while, and he also worked part-time doing construction. Later he was a substitute teacher and then a special education teacher. He took me to his classroom a lot, and that was always interesting and fun. I think that led me into education as a career. He was the one who asked me how my day went because Mom was often working. She had a regular job and he was a presence there at home when we lived in Oregon.

When I was twelve, we moved from Oregon to Arizona. One of the things that made it more difficult was that I was going from elementary school to a new junior high school not knowing anybody. The other thing was that Michael started working fulltime as a teacher in a district where he's actually now assistant superintendent. I wouldn't see my parents until 6:30 or 7:00 at night, so I went from having him at home to being a latchkey kid. This made that whole time much more difficult.

When I was seventeen, my mom and Michael got divorced. That split up was really hard, especially on my sister Lois, who was twelve. As difficult as it was, I was emotionally ready to deal with it. Michael made a concerted effort to spend time with Lois and me. We would go and play pool on the weekend. Even though it was difficult, he wanted to provide some stability. One of the ways he wanted to keep a relationship with me was to allow me to use his car, which was fine with me.

My dad wasn't involved in my day-to-day struggles and challenges. I don't think he got to know me that well, and I didn't get to know him that well. He didn't feel comfortable calling my mom's house to ask to speak with me. There was tension about that. We would exchange Christmas gifts, but other than a couple of weeks around my birthday and Easter break (which happens around my birthday), and infrequent calls a month or two before my visit to plan what we would do, there was little contact.

Compared to his relationships with his other sons, my relationship with my dad is still distant. There's a gap there. It lacks development. He has had information about me, but he hasn't seen how those experiences have really shaped me into who I am. When you have a relationship with a child, there's some development that you shouldn't miss, for example, you shouldn't miss the years between six and nine. You can't get those years back. There are things with my dad that should have happened that would have made the relationship closer. For example, I knew my dad worked in Sacramento, but I didn't know exactly what he did. If I had grown up with him, that would not have been a surprise to me. There's a whole bunch of "who you really are" things that I don't know about him. If you spend enough time with someone, the important things come out.

My relationship with my dad was in the background, like a lifeline out to some other place. That connection gave me the security that I did have another home, a place I could call home even if it wasn't always comfortable. I was pretty flexible in seeing that both sides were all part of my family, including my dad, my stepmom, and my brothers.

Two Moms

I don't know if I had heard about Cinderella's evil stepmother when I met my stepmom, but I remember coldness. Not like frigid coldness, but not the kind of warmth that you would expect in a family. I knew that this was a relationship that was going to be challenging. Unlike Michael, who was trying very hard to be a father, the effort wasn't there with her. But I thought, "I'm just the three-week kid. This is the way it is; I'm just here for three weeks, and she is just someone I have to deal with to be here with my dad."

I realize that Cindy was very uncomfortable with herself in ways and took it out on other people, and I think that contributed to my own discomfort with myself. That's been an issue for me as a person. She said things to me that were both compliments and cutting remarks. Always cutting. My mom has said a number of things that have been complimentary and cutting also, but she's also demonstrated so much support and love over the years. But Cindy, for anything good she did, there was always at least something bad that she did too. Life would have been a lot worse if I had lived with my dad and Cindy.

Cindy was very undecided about wanting to be a parent. I never heard her say, "Hey, it's really great to have you here; thanks for coming." Never really heard those words. There wasn't any positive expression. The lack of positivity was really solid. A classic scene is Dad coming to pick me up at the train station. We come in the house and Cindy is sitting on the couch. I say, "Hi, Cindy!" and she says, "Hello, Sam." She wasn't waiting at the door, making a special deal of that. My visit was something that was just going to be. She didn't really try and make me feel welcome in the house. My brother's and my relationships with our dad were always hard for her. We threatened her, and there were lots of ways that she would make him choose between her and us.

We had a typical pattern. First, we would try to do something together as a family. Then there would be tensions and disagreements. I would get in trouble with Cindy for God knows what. Then my dad and Cindy would have some disagreement about it, and later, all the boys would go do something together. I always enjoyed the visits more when Cindy wasn't around. I have very few memories of us all doing enjoyable things together. Some things we did together were okay, but there were few things that were enjoyable.

I see her as a cautionary tale. She was an alcoholic. I figured out what an alcoholic was, as opposed to some kind of mysterious, demonized character like a drug addict, when I was fifteen. I could see her use. Just about every dinner I've ever had with my dad, he's had a beer or glass of wine, but I can't think of any time I've ever seen my dad actually get drunk. But Cindy would have a beer or drink with dinner, and then she would also have a drink after dinner, or sometimes more than one drink. She drank hard liquor in a glass, so it was difficult to know how much she was consuming. I remember visiting when I was in my late teens and all of a sudden it made sense—the evenings watching TV and her sometimes-odd behavior. All of a sudden it just kind of clicked. That really helped explain a lot. In my mind I always pictured her as part of my family. I had a big family, but she was always a strained piece in there.

However, my mom was always there for me. She took communicating with me seriously. She wouldn't hold back just because I was young. My mom was always honest, a "keep it real" person. She was very loving and alive. Sometimes hugging my dad seemed a little odd because I didn't do it a lot. Hugging my mom never feels wrong. It feels natural.

My mom is a doctor, and when I was young , she had a practice in Ashland, Oregon. She had a male receptionist. I learned good gender roles; I learned that people could do anything. Our mother is amazing. She's accomplished great things, built houses by herself, taken on crazy projects and made them happen just through the combination of intelligence and will. But at the same time she has insecurities that she has passed on. Michael built up her confidence. And that was really good

Brothers and Sister

My siblings and stepsiblings played important roles. Roland, my brother, was six years older than me and had a memory of our parents being together. My dad and mom really fought over him, and some of those experiences probably damaged his self-confidence.

His experience with the stepmother/stepfather thing was much worse than mine. Roland went back and forth a lot but lived with my dad primarily. My dad's household was his household, his home. He had a horrible time living there. I never heard my brother say anything positive or loving toward Cindy, or her say anything positive or loving about him.

I remember one time when I visited my dad, Roland was grounded for the entire first week, and I couldn't play with him. That was really wrong. Maybe as a parent you have to do something, but not to the point of denying me my relationship with my brother. A lot of times I would see how difficult it was with my stepmom and brother and try not to do what he did.

Roland came to live with my mom in Oregon when he was in the eighth grade. I remember that when he first came, he really chafed at Michael's authority. He felt, "Forget it, I'm going to do what I want."

I felt like, "Hey I'm five years old. I don't have a close father figure, and here's Michael and he's all right." But Roland felt, "I have a dad, and you're not him, and you're not going to be him." My brother had a hard time with my closeness with Michael. Afterwards he regretted not having a closer relationship with Michael, and he tells me I'm lucky to have had a better relationship. But he's also closer to my dad, so there are trade-offs.

My stepbrother Owen is one year older than me, so we would hang out. Cindy adopted Owen before she and my father were married. And then my dad adopted him, too. As we got older, I began to do more athletic stuff. He wasn't as athletic and kind of out-of-shape. We would go places together and watch television together. We didn't have much contact with each other when I wasn't there. Owen would get that icy stare of doom just as often or more than I would, so I kind of thought Cindy was rough on everybody.

My stepbrother Terry was born in 1976, when I was about five. Cindy always had the impression that we were going to take advantage of him because we were a little bit older. So there was a kind of victim thing. Terry was always saying that we were picking on him. So I ended up oftentimes hanging out more with Owen. But it seemed like Terry was Cindy's baby, so I guess she tried to protect him from our "bad influences" or rough ways.

My half-sister Lois was born in 1977 when I was six. She is Michael's and my mom's daughter. She calls me big brother still.

Grandparents

My grandmother on my mom's side is the lynchpin of our family, the main grandma. She is an amazing, funny, dynamic woman. I visited her house a lot as a child. She always understood people. There was no problem between two people that she couldn't figure out something to say to make it better. She could break it down. There wasn't much that I wouldn't talk with her about.

Michael's parents would also visit. Both are dead now. They were Grandma and Grandpa Daley. Even after Michael and Mom were divorced, Grandma sent me a card saying that I was still her grandkid, and that was good. It always seemed to me as a child that they drank a lot.

Now

My experience as a stepchild has affected me in good and not so good ways. There was a woman who loved me, who was my mom, who sometimes said things that weren't good for my confidence, but who always loved me and always came through. And then there was another woman, who was my stepmom, who could turn on me in an instant with completely crazy justifications for things that I did or didn't do. Nothing was ever good enough for her. Today I think I carry a fear of rejection. I guess it does hurt to be rejected by your stepmom. I'm past that.

She's out of my life. But I came into her life wanting her to like me. I think a child wants everybody to love them.

I'm twenty-nine now, and I've always been a little behind in terms of relationships. I didn't really date in high school. I didn't have a serious relationship until after college. And even now, I have real issues about relationships. I have a hard time maintaining them. I'm more of a drop 'em kind of guy. It's easier for other people to be fluid with people. I'm always accepting in my mind that whoever it is may leave my life without warning, whether I want it to happen or not. That makes it harder for me. I'd love to have kids and get married but it takes a lot of work and sometimes I don't feel up to putting in that kind of work. But I think I would make a good dad. I would like to try it out. It's an eighteen-year plus commitment. There's no return policy

Often I feel like I don't have firm footing. I'm a teacher, and I can reflect about what goes on in the classroom and make my practice as a teacher better. I've played basketball, and I can analyze my game and improve what I need to do. But in terms of relationships, when things get difficult I think, "Forget it." I know how I feel about people, but I don't feel like I know what other people feel about me. It's a footing issue. In high school, that was really a scary thing. But now I have enough self-confidence to know that if people don't think I'm cool, it doesn't matter. I don't give a bleep about that. I can brush off criticism. The world is a big place.

I don't worry about table manners now, but that used to be an issue. I went out last night and there was a point when I was uncomfortable, and there was a point at which I became comfortable. Part of that moving to comfortable was getting over the fear that I'm going to get the icy cold stare for eating my food messily, for being a slob. Self-assured people don't worry about their table manners.

I think I understand the challenges my students face in dealing with different family situations. If I had grown up with parents who had stayed married and if I'd had the model TV family structure, it would be more difficult for me to put myself in the shoes of kids who are having trouble with their stepmom or can't see their dad. Been there; done that.

I like to think that as difficult as my life was, it has taught me to deal with loss. My life has been turned upside down more than once, I've moved more than once, and I've grown from this. I can deal with change.

I see family as more inclusive than exclusive. My mom hasn't remarried but Michael has. His wife Lucy is also divorced, also has kids from another family. At Christmas time, Michael wants his kids—Roland, myself, and Lois—to come over and be with Lucy and her kids. And we're all family I guess. Technically, he's an ex-stepdad. So you need to be fluid about your idea of family. There are blood relationships, and then there's people who've been in the same house or houses, or who have been part of the houses, as it were. I guess that's the way I see it. But when I think about what a family should do, it's to facilitate the betterment of everybody who's in it.

I have never thought about how these experiences shaped my life in much detail. I've experienced a lot of personal growth in the past few years. It's been really good to look at this. You can't blame people for how things were. About 99.9 percent of us have lives that are better than some and worse than others. Few people have relationships with stepparents that are as bad as the one I had with my stepmother. But there are things that were good in my relationship with my stepdad. I can ignore the one and hold on to the other.

Sam's Advice for Stepparents

Nurture the relationship.

When you don't live with a child, but he or she is expected to be part of your family, it is not realistic to assume that the child will pick things up by osmosis. If you are going to live together, even for three weeks a year, you need to pay attention to having a relationship. This means maintaining communication during the time you don't see the child. If you want to build a relationship, you need on-going dialogue.

Tell the child right from the start, "I'm so and so. I'm going to be an important person in your dad's life, and hopefully I would also like to be an important person in your life. And, of course, I want you to get to know me a little bit. From here we're going to move forward." When I would go to visit my dad, there wasn't ever a time to hang out with Cindy, to see what she did, to get to know her separate from my dad. That would have helped our relationship.

The stepparent shouldn't try to please the other parent as their motivation for getting along with the stepkids. That's not genuine. You have to value your relationship with your stepchildren independent from your relationship with your spouse. Either you have an interest or you don't. You can't pretend. Kids will see through that. My relationship with Michael didn't end when my mom and he split up. That was because we made an effort. I have two dads; one is a bonus dad.

Just try and be a good parent.

Part of the word stepparent is parent. Don't worry about being a stepparent or whether your stepkids will listen to you or like you. The authority, the influence, and the meaningfulness will come from the fact that you are there. My stepdad didn't have to say, "Well, you know, your dad's not here, so I'm going to be your father." He was just there for me.

Michael didn't pass the buck on things.. He took on father roles. For example, there was that talk about sex. He talked to me about that because I was a teenage male: somebody's got to. It would have sounded even funnier from my dad because he didn't have the inside track on my day-to-day life. I wasn't telling Michael all my business at that point, but he at least had some idea.

Be respectful of the other parent.

If you are the stepfather, recognize that there is another father; if you are the stepmother; recognize that there is a mother. You can't be that person and should not try to be a substitute for that person. Your relationship should be important on its own terms. You shouldn't say, "Your lousy lay-about dad isn't here, but I'm here." You can't build yourself up by putting down the other. Give space to the children to figure out their own relationships. It's not like a pie that you have to divide; the pie can get bigger.

Sam's Advice to Parents

Plan visits carefully . . .

As much as possible, make sure that you're sending the message that this time together is special. Just coming to visit, coming to watch your regular routine, would be wrong. That's what you do when you have the other forty-nine weeks out of the year. Make plans beforehand and involve your kids in the process.

My dad would take off work to be with me. Not everybody has this luxury, but let your child know you'll be doing special things together. My dad would cancel work on Friday so we could go on a three-day camping trip on the weekend. Do those kinds of things.

. . . but not like a vacation.

What wouldn't work is always going to Disneyland. Don't make everything super special because that's not real. I liked it when my dad would ask me to come to his work. I would come by at the end of his day and catch him in his work mode a little bit and see the transition out of that. That helped me understand him a little bit. I liked seeing his office, where he worked and what he did. I found that interesting. Then, during the months we weren't together, I had a point of reference.

Regular communication: keep track of what is going on in your child's life.

Keep a file. Write down what's going on and then remember to ask about it when you call. For example, "The last time we talked, you said that you really thought your math class sucked; do you still feel that way?" When you live with someone, you don't have to do that because you know what goes on each day. But when you don't, there could have been a major event that had its beginning, middle, and end already, and it's already moved on. And you don't know about it.

There were key events that my dad missed that you can't track without asking some general questions and following up again. As a high school teacher, I know teenagers aren't necessarily very forthcoming about what is bothering them or what's really important. Most kids don't say that out front. But there is so much that is important; there are so many things that are going on right beneath the surface, that you have to have some way of getting that out, or allowing that to come out. It has to be a conscious effort. Otherwise, it is snippets, a little packet here, little packet there, and it doesn't bring together a whole picture.

Like, for example, I had a lot of problems in junior high when I moved to Arizona. I had an ongoing beef with this one guy for basically the rest of high school. It only stopped when he went to juvenile hall for a while and was expelled from school. I'd get into a fight with him and then get jumped by him and his gang. Those kinds of things aren't things I necessarily wanted to just open up about. So if a kid says he got into a fight or whatever, ask him about it again in another month. "Everything cool, everything okay? Are you still getting into fights or are things better?"

Show that you can work together for the sake of the child.

There was always a difference between the households. There should have been more communication about these differences. I didn't get the sense that my parents talked to each other about me. It kind of surprised me when my mom said, "Well, I've been talking with your dad about college and we figured that your dad will pay for your first two years, and then I'll pay for your last two years." That was the only time I remember them talking about me. I got the image then that they had actually talked about it and made the decision together. I was happy that they had done that because it seemed like they had bothered to coordinate something besides just flight times and arrivals. Parents should realize that whenever they say, "I spoke with your dad and we both agree," that whatever comes after that is going to carry much more weight.

In high school, I was competing in a tournament and my mom and dad both showed up. This was a month or two after their separation. They were on a better swing. They weren't yelling at each other. To see them sitting together, even though I had no illusions about their getting back together, made me feel better. This didn't happen that often, but when it did, it was really meaningful.

It sends a message to the children that they're important, important enough to both parents that when it comes to their children's needs, they can work things out, even if it's as simple as sending a check. If the parents can't talk about how to split the cost of summer camp tuition, what happens when a more challenging problem appears? Knowing that the conversation is taking place is important to a child.

When this doesn't happen, the child ends up having to pick sides and that is very uncomfortable. Even if you do it only once, you end up losing. You don't get closer to one parent because you picked them. You end up losing the relationship with the other parent. It's a road you don't want to go down.

Bring the families together.

When the children are going from one house to the other, try and bring the families together. Maybe meet at a restaurant and eat together before exchanging the child. Not seeing everybody together made me think of family as split and separated. When my parents would drop me off, I felt like I was in one of those movies where they're exchanging hostages, with me on one side of the bridge, my other parent on the other side, and I would walk across.

One of my favorite pictures is of my brother Roland, my brother Owen, and my grandmother (my mom's mom) together. I would have liked having my sister know my brothers. I know that for a while my mom and my dad really didn't trust each other and were struggling with custody. That made things difficult and very tense, but I think it would have made everybody feel a little better to see everybody together.

I had the sense that other people's families were much closer. I never got a chance to see all the people in our family together much. Actually, I never saw my mom and Cindy in the same room. And I don't think they ever talked. I remember one Christmas we were driving through Sacramento. We stopped, and Michael went in to exchange presents with my dad and stepmom and then came back out. That was it. There was no idea that we were going to try and do anything together whatsoever.

Intervene when necessary.

My father was too passive around my stepmom. I was in punishment more in those three weeks than the rest of the year. My dad should have intervened. He should have been more pro-active. We never sat down when we were all calm to talk about how things should be.

Sam's Advice for Stepchildren

There are no words that I can give that will protect or arm a stepchild. It's up to the parents to do that. Five-year-old kids can't figure these things out or make things right.

■■■■■■■■■■■■■■■■■■■■■■■■■■■■■■■ ■ ■

Maya

Maya is in her early thirties. Her parents divorced when she was four. Her father remarried soon after, and her mother remarried when Maya was twelve. Her mother is now divorced, and her father is still married. Maya has a brother, and a half-brother and half-sister. She is a writer.

Maya's Story

My parents separated when I was three and divorced when I was four. I don't remember meeting my stepmom, but it was shortly after the divorce. It's funny how that happens, how it's just all of a sudden there. I don't remember being introduced to her. I don't remember them ever getting married, just knowing that they were married and one day coming across a wedding picture.

Both of my parents come from alcoholic, uneducated, working-class families. My dad comes from the east side of the city, Mafia type. Their language is kind of like that of the characters on *NYPD Blue*, the fat guy with a clipped tongue. That's how they talk. He comes from a love-repressed background and is unable to express his emotions and therefore is unable to relate to his family in any way other than financially. My mom is from a totally rural background. She is a whole basket case herself. I think she might have had a nervous breakdown at one time, but I'm not sure because I don't remember any of that at all. I know that my childhood was sad. I try to go back there, and there are huge blank chunks where I lose two years.

Life with Mom

My brother and I lived mostly with my mom. For breakfast we would have orange juice with raw egg and wheat germ. Healthy things. We didn't have sugar or cereal; we weren't allowed things like that. We had a vegetable with every dinner. We had actual food. And we would do things like read books. She read to us every single night. We would go to the museum. There were constant activities, more eclectic things. We weren't allowed to watch television. But we were latchkey kids, so we would come home, watch TV, and scrounge for anything that had sugar. When we would hear the garage door open, we would shut off the TV and run. We had chores, a list of things to do. And we would make up things to play. We would hold haunted houses in our garage and chase each other around with knives, kitchen knives. We were wild—we had these wild imaginations because we were read to; we were raised with imagination.

But I wanted my mom to be different. I wanted her to be a real mother, and she wasn't really capable of that. She could be fun and play-like, but she just was not nurturing. She didn't know how. She was too up and down and in and out. Getting the guy was always the most important thing, more so than her kids. The guys always came before the kids. She just went from relationship to relationship to relationship. I didn't like any of the guys she dated. And also, she would date problematic guys, and often way younger guys. They didn't know how to be around a kid, let alone me. They were just dicks. And there was major competition between the guys and us kids.

Oh, I was awful. I was like a terror, stubborn and mean. I remember one time chasing after my mom's car screaming because I had wanted to go along, but she didn't even see me. I went to my room and just screamed and sobbed hysterically. And this guy was there and he was trying to get me to calm down and I was screaming. I wouldn't even acknowledge his presence. I was really dramatic, but I honestly felt that bad.

My mom married a dick named Lenny when I was in seventh grade and stayed married to him for way too long, about four years. I never developed any relationship with him at all, never. This guy was bad and my mother couldn't see that. He was a raging alcoholic, and everything about him turned out to be a lie. He had all these elaborate stories about how he went to school, and all of it was a lie. He didn't have any money. He took my mom for everything; he was a true con artist.

They would fight and chase each other around. Before she married him, she would call 911 on him. I remember being so embarrassed that 911 came to my house. One day I looked out on the balcony, and there they were in a major fight. He had blood and scratch marks on him, there was a broken tennis racket, and the police were on their way. And you know, being a kid, I was protective of my mom. But I remember thinking, "She's so stupid. God, she's an idiot." I wanted to shake her.

Today I can see her marriage to him was a fork in my road. I had been kind of interested in science, and that is when kids first study science. However, we were fighting so much that I sort of shut down and I didn't do or learn anything, you know. And if life had been different, maybe today I would be a doctor. But I stopped trying.

Life with Dad

My brother and I went to my dad's and stepmom's every weekend after I was in second grade. I don't remember that starting; it just seems like going there on the weekends was my whole life, and it was so annoying.

Our dad would pick us up on Friday afternoon after

he was done with work and we were done with school, and we would drive to his house. When you're a kid, the drive is forever. It seemed like six hours, but with traffic maybe it took forty-five minutes or an hour. We would be there for the weekend, but our father was working, so we would be with his wife. We would hang out with our cousins or go shopping. That's what we did. He would drive us back either late Sunday night or early Monday morning.

At our dad's house, the TV was on the whole time. We would go to the store on the first night and get all kinds of candy and those mini-donuts, and the whole weekend we would inhale candy and hoard it. It was like a party. So even today, I don't have anything in common with those people. They're just regular, really middle-class people. Dinner for them is frozen fried chicken in the oven. They didn't have table manners. It was so different from my mom's.

For a long time I didn't think about the visits to my dad's because I didn't know there was a choice, that is until roller-skating started, which was in junior high. Then I started to go to my friend's house and realized that my life was different. I didn't have many friends, only cousins, because I wasn't home enough to form friendships. I didn't want to go to my dad's, but I had to go. Because of roller-skating, I was starting to make friends, and I wanted to stay with them. I remember my parents saying, "Well, you can bring your friends with you to your dad's," but I didn't want to. I wanted to stay there in my house. Then it got to be really icky

Our stepmother was sort of like our babysitter. We thought she was nice. The relationship was friendly. It wasn't motherly. You know how you have people who are your friends, but they really don't know you, they're more like an acquaintance? You see them when you go to work, but you wouldn't hang out with them on the weekend. It was like that. That is how I would describe her. But then when she had her children, that was it. All of a sudden, we took a back seat; all of a sudden, we're in the trunk. It was interesting how that transition came about, and it would become even more and more severe as her kids grew up.

I went to their family functions, which was so dumb. You know how you do things and you realize it's just not it? You grow into your own person. People will tell you, "Oh, you need to be with your family." I don't think so. Sometimes people are just not meant to be part of that family. They're meant to break a cycle.

I don't really speak to my dad and stepmother anymore. My relationship with my father is a check folded into a card at Christmas and on my birthday. Once my stepmother sent me a letter saying that I was ungrateful and that I only came around for the money. When it was time to go to college, I wasn't really ready, but she sent money and told me I had to go, that it was part of the agreed-upon arrangement. My mother had hardly received any child support, but the arrangement was that he would take care of medical expenses and pay for our educations. My stepmother said I had to take that money because we had grown up not really having anything because he was saving it all for our college educations. I sent back the money with a letter saying that I never asked for this anyway. I would have enjoyed a father. I was so angry. And I could tell that he was upset with her for doing that. Then over the years, she would try to approach me. He never would though, never once. And maybe six years went by, and I didn't have any contact with him.

Not long ago, I was in the Twin City area, and my stepmother called. She was really hesitant, walking on glass, like someone who didn't know me at all. "I was wondering if you would want to come to dinner." I didn't want to go, but I agreed. My mom conned me into it. I knocked on the door. My dad was sitting at the table, his back to the door. He just kind of turned around and looked. Didn't get up, didn't let me in or anything. And I'm thinking, "Why am I even here?" He didn't speak throughout the whole dinner. Nothing.

Siblings

I was my brother's mother. I was my mother's mother also. I sort of took over. But I was mean, kind of bossy, because I didn't know how to be a mother. I was only ten. He was wild. I remember one time he was in the kitchen and he just destroyed it. He made pudding with the blender and the cover wasn't on. The kitchen literally exploded. I don't know what he was doing in there; it was just this huge mess and he was watching TV. He just left it! I screamed, "Joe, pick this up." And he said he didn't do it. "Who did it? We're the only people here. You know?" And he would just ignore me. I remember thinking that boys are gross, and they're not like girls. When he peed, I'd say, "Joe, wash your hands." I was always getting him to pick up his stuff and wash his hands after he went to the bathroom.

I don't really have that much of a relationship with him today. He went to live with my dad when he was a freshman in high school. That is a bummer because he would have turned out differently, extremely differently had he not. My mom had him in acting class, and he was really outgoing. But she couldn't handle him, like she couldn't handle me, so she shipped him off because she was just so unstable.

I remember him trying out for this musical, *Oliver*. All of these kids are up there and they have to sing a song from a musical, and Joe gets up there and he starts singing *Beth* from Kiss, this huge rock 'n' roll group. It was so funny. I was peeing my pants, thinking, "Oh my God, here's someone who's functional. And he's singing *Beth*, and he's totally in his own world, and he doesn't even get it that these kids are singing *Godspell* or whatever." Oh, it was so funny. So that was his personality, really outgoing. And then he went to live with my dad.

I also have a half-brother and half-sister. My relationship with my half-siblings is not as intense as the one I have with my brother because there is a ten- or thirteen-year age difference. My brother and I are closer in age and have been through more together. You know sometimes you can combine the families and you do it so there's no difference or anything. But because we were coming from two very different backgrounds, there were a whole lot of differences. And when people say, "Do you have a brother or sister?" I say that I have a brother. And I know some families where they have half-brothers and half-sisters and they're just like another sibling. "Oh yes, I have this brother and this brother." With me, it isn't like that. And even to this day I don't really talk to them.

And there was Grandmother

I was close to my grandmother, but she died Easter time when I was in the eighth grade. She was a motivator. She knew what I liked, whereas my mother didn't. We saw her at least once a week. My grandmother provided the stability in my life, which is probably why I got really bad because she died at the most intense time. I think that when a parent is not 100 percent available and a grand-parent is present in the child's life, it is only natural that the grandparent would play an important role. I believe my grandmother was important because I viewed her as an adult—responsible and competent.

Now

The stepchild experience has affected me in various ways. Throughout my life, I've had a lot of families adopt me. The family of one of my friends took me on their vacations with them. They were my family. I have that orphan quality. It's a sore subject with my mom that everybody wants to be my mom, but obviously she was not good at it.

I believe family should be like a job. That's sort of how I see it. When I have kids, let's say **if** I have kids, it's important to me that my husband and I sign a contract, not for marriage, but a contract that requires we stay together for eighteen years until the kid goes to college. I have an idea in my head of how I want to be a parent. I would set down rules, and I would be there for my children. We would sit down together, and I would make them do their homework. I would understand that they are kids and that every person is an individual. I'm just going to be there for them. Hands down, like an earth mother. An earth mother with no strings attached. You know the theory that if you love something, you let it go.

I'm extremely loyal, maybe like overly loyal. But, at the same time, I move really slowly. I'm really hesitant. I don't allow anyone to get close to me too fast. I keep my distance. I won't let anyone smother me, man or woman. I'm very private. Yet I'm open, and I'll tell you whatever, but at the same time I'm really private. I like to be in relationships, and at the same time I really need my privacy. I like to go out and I really enjoy people, but I need to also spend time with myself. I start to overload. Maybe it's because I grew up spending so much time with myself that I also need to be alone. I have that loner quality.

For the most part I trust people. Upon meeting someone, I'm pretty instinctual, I get a vibe. My parents aren't very trusting, and I think that's maybe what got them into trouble. But generally I give people the benefit of the doubt.

I'm extremely eclectic. I'm not normal. I'm a writer and I think that's maybe what I had to be. It's not like I consciously chose to be a writer; it just sort of happened because I have all these emotions inside of me. They're like my paints that I'm able to play with. And so if I need sadness, I have tons of it, and I can pull it up. And hopefully I can make the reader feel because I'm actually using real emotions. I have a lot of depth inside me that I can use. Emotions never go away.

Right now I'm ready to put the past behind me and move forward.

Maya's Advice for Stepparents

Treat all the children the same.

I just know that when my stepmom had her kids, they were hers and the selfishness came into play. If I were to be a stepmom, I'd try not to have segregation. Let's say my husband had kids, and let's say his kids did bounce back and forth between homes. The kids would still be equal, all the same, while they were under my roof. You know, if so and so is getting yelled at because his room is messy, so is so-and-so. I'm not going to give so-and-so a break because she's only here for the night. They would know they would all be treated the same.

Let stepchildren learn about each other.

Arrange for your children to visit your stepchild's home. Take them to see the stepchild's room. Then the kids sort of know what's going on, so they're not left in the dark. Otherwise, they don't have any idea what life is like when the kid is at the other house. It's just this strange person who comes over to visit on weekends. When you have friends, you go to your friend's house and you see what it looks like, and sometimes you play at their house.

Don't say bad things about the other parent.

Children want to think their parents are perfect. When you're a kid, you're in a fantasy world. Then there's this person coming into your fantasy world saying bad things about your parents. You don't tell that to a child. I'm sorry. That stuff is just too adult. It's just not nice. Because what can the child do? She's not in a position that she can do anything. If you're only five years old, you can't go and get your own job and say, "I'm out of here. I don't need to hear this." So it makes you schizophrenic internally.

Maya's Advice for Parents

Ask what the child thinks.

The family's a unit; everything has to work together in order for it to work. So you don't just bring someone in and say this is how it's going to be. Maybe you should ask, "What do you think about this person? Do you like him?" Because it's not just the mother that is marrying this guy; the whole family is marrying that guy. Children are not stupid. In most cases, they're smarter than their parents, and they have a certain instinct. Can't you just be friends with him or her and not get married? Have an affair on the side, and just don't tell anyone

Make a commitment to your children.

I would never have kids unless it's ideal. When you have kids, it's important to sign an eighteen-year contract. You made the commitment to have a kid; that's your job.

If things don't work out, you stay together. In the grand scheme of things, let's say the kid's five, what is thirteen more years? Time goes like that.

My normalcy ended when my parents split. Did you see the movie *Faithless*? It's about a divorce. It's a Swedish film made by Ingmar Bergman. They captured everything. It's about the selfishness of adults, people in general, but it happens to be the parents. And they have a fine relationship, nothing wrong with it. And the woman gets this craving to sleep with the best friend. So they give in to their selfishness, and they start having an affair. You know, they get all wrapped up in this and they feel guilty about the kid, but they don't do anything about it. There's this shot where they show the expression on the kid's face. It just shows everything. And you know at that moment, that kid's life is just ruined. It's just changed completely. Any sense of normalcy, or anything that this kid had is just—whew. I think you can be as selfish as you want, you can do whatever you want, but not if you're going to have kids. Then that becomes a job and a responsibility.

Stay in one house.

The switching back and forth is awful. Just let the kids stay in one house. I know it's going to be sad and hard and everything, but in the long run, it's going to be better on the kid. I just think that's so selfish of parents. You can visit the kids, take them out to lunch or whatever, but I think it's better for them to stay in one house. You don't take baby bears from one place to the other day after day. They stay there until they learn how to walk and they go off on their own. Why do the parents have to volley the child? You know, you can't divide a human being. I have this image of a Barbie doll; you pull on Barbie's legs, and they're going to snap off.

Don't turn your child into a caregiver.

Seeing that the parent is sad, the child goes into the position of caregiver. The child takes over and tries to make the parent happy. Instinctually it happens. And then they don't get to experience their own sadness until later.

Make your contact real.

I remember for a while my dad used to call every day. "What'd you have for lunch? It was the same question, "What'd you have for lunch? What did you do today?" I mean it was just so lame; give it a rest. And I knew it was forced because as a kid, when you hear the same question over and over, you know that he doesn't have anything to talk about. Why bother? He was trying to express himself, but he didn't know how. He tried, and then I think he got tired. There was a point where he let it go. I'm aware of that.

Maya's Advice for Stepchildren
I can't think of anything that would help.

■ ■

Richard

Richard is thirty-two years old. His parents divorced when he was fourteen. Richard's father remarried when he was sixteen, and his mother remarried when he was eighteen. After the divorce, he left San Diego, where he had lived with his mother and father, and moved to Lake Tahoe with his mother. Several years after his mother remarried, he moved back to San Diego to live with his father and stepmother. He has two sisters and one half-brother, the son of his father and stepmother. Richard is an actor, and he has been in a committed relationship for three years.

Richard's Story

When my parents got a divorce, my sisters and I moved with my mom to Lake Tahoe while my dad stayed in San Diego. I think my mom just wanted to get as far away as possible so we packed all of our things, said good-by to our friends and family, and moved. Other than moving away from my grandparents, one of the hardest things was saying good-by to the pets. My dog stayed with my dad, my fish was flushed, and my mom made me let my hamsters go by a river—like they would ever survive!

Once we got to Lake Tahoe, life changed drastically. I was suddenly "the man of the house." I registered myself for ninth grade and looked for a job. I started high school with all these strangers—very scary. I was just starting to come to terms with being gay. I was "the new guy," and as a result, I got beaten up regularly at school. I took care of my sisters in the evening, making dinner, helping them with their homework, and getting them to bed.

Later that year, in 1981 my dad told me that he and his girlfriend were getting married. He sent airfare for me to attend the wedding, but he wasn't able to afford to get my sisters there. It was a strange wedding. It was my dad, but in so many ways I didn't feel like I was a part of what was going on. There was very little family from my dad's side, and I didn't know many of my soon-to-be stepmother's family. I wasn't in the wedding party or asked to be involved in any way. I was like "Hey, I'm the first born!" I was expecting to be best man or do a reading—something. When they started the wedding pictures, they didn't even have me come up and be in them. I don't think a lot of the people even knew I was his son or if they did, I was a past that a lot of people didn't want to acknowledge: my dad's former marriage with three kids. I just sat alone in the church, making small talk with a lot of strangers. It was a pretty awful wedding.

My mom married someone a few years later. I met him on their second date and I know it sounds funny, but I just knew he was a bad guy. Years later it turns out I was right. They dated for a very short time and then set a date to marry. His brother and son came to stay with us, and we got to know him and his family a great deal more. His children didn't like him at all. His brother, my new uncle, was clearly on drugs and my mother seemed oblivious to it all. They had a very small service and after there was a champagne reception. I felt so trapped and powerless in the situation, I drank every glass of champagne I could find, and that night was the first time I ever got drunk.

Once we'd settled into our new living situation, it became clear that it was impossible. Quite honestly, I had no respect for the guy. He had no work ethic, made really stupid choices, and insisted that he be called "Dad." For a brief time, I worked at McDonald's and then he got a job there too—now we were peers at work! Somehow, my mother didn't seem to notice his strange behavior, the way he was treating my sisters, and no matter what, she always took his side regardless of the issue. I began cutting classes, shoplifting, and hitting my sisters. I had a bag packed in my room so at any time I would be ready to run away.

It became so unlivable, I decided to call my dad and ask him if I could move back to San Diego and live with him and my new stepmom. I bought a car, packed all my things, and said my good-bys. My mother and I were on bad terms. She was angry I was leaving, especially to live with my dad. She didn't say good-by.

Stepparents

I think I tried really hard to get my stepfather to like me. I think that's a theme in my growing up—trying to survive by being as likeable as possible, being small and unnoticeable. Sounds like a good strategy but it didn't work for long because I'm not so small, I'm not so unnoticeable and I have always had a strong sense of right and wrong. When I was a kid, my anger and frustration came out in creative and destructive ways. I was shoplifting, cutting school constantly, and becoming increasingly violent with my sisters and, at the same time, I wrote radio plays, poetry, and songs day and night. I tried to do anything I could to create some control of my environment. I'd even save up my money and paint and repaint my room several times a month.

As I said, as soon as I met my stepfather, I knew he was bad news. I knew right away, but there was nothing I could do. That's who my mom picked and that's who we got. I think I just decided that in order to survive, I had to work with what I had and so did my sisters. It turns out we were right—he was bad news.

He was an ordained minister, unable to secure a position in the church, so he was paid a small honorarium as a music minister. Essentially, he remained jobless for most of their twelve-year marriage. From our perspective as kids, we saw a man with terrible judgment, and painfully isolated. All the while our mother would support his every decision and stand by his side. What we didn't know at the time was that he and his brother were drug addicts (cocaine). They were arrested and jailed several times, and on one occasion my mother bailed him out of jail, taking a second mortgage on the house. Towards the end, I found out that his father molested a member of our family. His father had violated all the women in their family and until that point had gone unreported and unpunished. We pressed charges, and later our family booked a counseling session so that we could begin to repair all that had been broken. The day before our appointment, my stepfather was gone. He left my mother a note. It seems he'd spent the previous week secretly taking money, packing a van, and tying up loose ends. In the night, he left California for Florida with the church secretary. Did I mention he was a minister?

In the beginning, I kind of liked my stepmother but she was hard to read; it was almost something like "Oh my gosh, this guy I married has three kids." She inherited three kids and a past that I don't think she wanted and she resented it. When us kids would visit her and my dad, there were a lot of comments like "When are you guys leaving? I want you out of the house." It was all said in a "joking" tone, but we all hated it.

She was often a really sweet person, but she had her insecurities. She and I would always have run-ins; she was only about twelve years older than I was so we were a little like siblings. She would say, "Don't talk about your dad being an alcoholic or that he was in AA. I don't want my family to know that." She wanted to rein in any information about the past that she didn't like or want her family to know about.

The big moment with her and me was when I came out to her as a gay man. She figured it out and confronted me, and when I confirmed it was true, she had a really bad reaction. The short version is she said she "wouldn't wish that hell on anyone" and then told me to move out of the house and have no contact with my baby brother. If I did as I was told, she wouldn't tell my dad. It was so shocking, and I was so afraid to lose my dad that I did just that. I moved out. My dad never knew why. Luckily, my brother and I stayed inseparable. My dad and I continued to be close, and years later I told him and my mother that I was gay. He was totally fine with it and has never had any problem with it at all. My stepmom and I have never talked about any of this. I'm sure we will one of these days.

It's always been hard for her to be openly loving and nice to us kids. Her way of showing love is to make fun of you, to be boisterous and rude and inappropriate. I think all of us kids have gotten used to it, and as she's gotten older, much of it has softened too.

Mom and Dad

My mom and I were really close until we moved to Lake Tahoe. When they divorced, I was on "her side." I picked sides. I felt I had to. I had been in on her conversations with my grandmother on how bad her marriage was, how horrible my dad was, and the ultimate decision to leave him. When they broke up, she came to my room and had me help her pack my dad's suitcase. I remember being so overwhelmed with emotion and responsibility, and missing my dad so much.

Later, after the divorce and her new marriage, we fought a lot. We fought about my stepdad, my sisters, everything. I rebelled a lot. She wouldn't let me go anywhere. I always had to stay home, take care of my sisters, and work at home. My mom and stepdad decided I should get a job to pay rent. I was expected to pay for college, schoolbooks—it was all on me. That was a really big thing to deal with, not having any support, paying my family to stay at my own home, and then later, seeing other people plan for college and go away while I kept working. I've had a hard time getting close to my mom again. She's very religious, conservative, and so hard to understand sometimes. I remember her as fun, laughing, and silly when I was a boy. All of that changed, and her life became so hard for her. I love her so much, and I know she did the best she could at the time, but yeah, we're not really close.

My relationship with my dad has grown closer and closer as we've grown older. It was hard for him to get close, and I'm impressed that he has gotten as far as he has. Growing up, I had a lot of fun with him; we did a lot of hunting, fishing, and road trips together. It's when I started getting into middle school and didn't want to go hunting, didn't want to go on trips all the time, that things changed. I think there was some awareness that "my son might be gay" so he spent a lot of time trying to change that. "You're going to shoot that gun and you're going to shoot twenty ducks." That would make me "a man."

When I see his relationship with the rest of our family, I realize that I have a great relationship with him. Some time after the divorce, I had a chance to talk to him about a lot of things that made me mad at him when I was growing up. He apologized and we really got to start over. Now if I have a problem, he'll talk about anything; he's a great listener, incredibly funny, and the storyteller of all storytellers. More and more, we can openly share with each other; he can talk about how proud of me he is, how much he loves me, and I can do the same with him.

Siblings

I have two younger sisters and a much younger half-brother. Before the divorce, my relationship with my sisters was great. I mean great. We would play all the time and not with toys but outside, setting up theaters, schools, and offices, all kinds of imaginary places and games. Both of my sisters were outgoing and really fun and adventurous. We put on skits, played store and bank. We never really needed toys; we would transform the bedrooms into shops, the house into a castle, the backyard into a palace.

Because of their ages, my sisters didn't know why our parents got a divorce. They don't even remember there being problems. They just know that suddenly we up and moved one day. So they have had a whole set of problems and issues that I didn't have. It's heartbreaking what they went through. They really went from a wonderful family situation to a really bad one. They didn't get the breaks that I did in some ways because I was older, and as soon as I could, I escaped.

During the years in Tahoe, it's really sad what happened. Here I was a freshman in high school, cutting school every day, smoking cigarettes, shoplifting, feeling totally trapped because I was in charge—I was the dad. I couldn't go anywhere, couldn't have any friends, mainly because my mom didn't want me out of the house. She wanted me there all the time. I was making dinner, cleaning the house, and in on all the financial troubles. I was completely overwhelmed by it all, so I took it out on my sisters. I would get violent and hit them. Yeah, there were good times too, but I'm not too proud of how it all went down. I beat up a few kids who gave my sisters a hard time and protected them a lot, but I was pretty out of control.

There came a point where I had so much guilt about it all that I had to apologize for all of the abuse in Lake Tahoe. My sisters had a chance to get angry with me and tell me what it was like for them. I heard what I did, apologized, and eventually I got to tell them what my life had been like. Why I did that to them and how out of control my life was, the physical abuse that I'd gotten from Mom and Dad that they'd sort of noticed but forgotten about. They started to remember all the times that I was beaten, all the times that we would go clothes shopping and they would both get things, but I wouldn't. All at once we, the three of us, came to a really clear understanding of what was done to us and why we did what we did to each other. We had a chance to apologize and come to understand and respect who we were. In the end, the apology I gave to my sisters was so freeing, to me as well as to them. It sort of let us all off the hook and gave us a chance to start over.

As for my half-brother, he came after all of this. He was born after I moved back with my dad and stepmom. I really adored him. How could you not fall in love with this amazing baby boy? I took care of him; it was like he was MY kid. I was twenty years old when he was born, and he went everywhere with me. I was like his dad in a way, or a live-in uncle. I babysat him, showed him all these great cartoons I grew up on and films, and I sang to him. Later, my sisters had time to get close to him, and now, the four of us are close. He had a great experience growing up, great dad, great mom, and this older brother and two sisters to take care of him.

Grandmother

My grandmother (my mom's mom) and I were close. She and my grandfather lived right up the street from us when my parents were still married. I would spend a lot of time with her talking about everything. In the late 1970's, she was diagnosed with emphysema and by the mid-80's was dying. It sounds pretty heavy but we did get really close. My granddad had a heart attack and died, and even though I was in high school, I started taking care of her. She had to have daily breathing treatments, she was bed-ridden, and she had an oxygen tank. She could do some things, but not much. She and I actually had a lot of fun. She was an artist and a writer so when she was really sick she would speak and I would write it all out, type it, and then we'd edit together. We would talk and talk. I think she taught me a lot about how to be a good man, how to be thoughtful.

Growing up, she was the only person to whom I could say; "This is what happened at school today. They called me 'fag' and I hate school, this guy hit me…" and I could really cry with her. She died at sixty-two years old. Days before she died, she was in the hospital and during my last visit she told me that it was okay to be a gay person and that no matter what, she loved me. After she died, I felt free. Nobody needed me any more and if they did, I just couldn't DO anymore. I packed my things and moved to New York to be an actor.

Lessons Learned

Through all of this experience, I have had a kind of resilience; I think all three of us kids do. After all I went through in my childhood, I came to believe I could survive anything. All those long conversations with my grandmother finally paid off in New York where I would remember a strong, working-class, farming family. I could tell myself, "I'm from good people. I'm a good person." And somehow I could talk myself out of feeling bad and continue to generate courage.

I'm not a dad yet, not sure if I will be but I'm a great brother and an awesome uncle, and I work with young people in an after-school program. Somehow, I've got all the patience in the world. That, and a good sense of humor. I learned how to deal with anger and disappointment and how to forgive.

I take risks. Other people tell me that I do things that they would never do. I have a lot of fear, but it doesn't stop me. Somehow, I just get up and do it. There are many areas I have a lot of fear about, but I am able to proceed anyway. I can make things work, and I know how to compromise. I survived my childhood, my uncle's early death, my stepfather, my stepmother, both my grandparents' deaths, AND New York.

So the negative part is that I've always fought with bouts of depression. Sometimes relationships are hard. I have felt a kind of desperation, like I really needed to get somebody and keep them so they wouldn't go away. I had a really bad habit early on of "Oh, you like me? Okay. Great. I'll date you." or "Do you think I'm okay? All right, fine. I'll marry you." That would be enough. I wasn't going out and finding the kind of person I really wanted. Then I would get into a relationship for I don't know how long and I would finally realize, "I can't stand this guy. What am I doing?" Then I would leave him and go on to the next person who said, "Oh, you have a nice smile," and I would say, "Really? Oh, okay, marry me." You know. And only the last five years have I really gotten a clue about that. I'm at the next level of actually getting what I want. I'm learning how to not be so accommodating. Mostly, I have a really good sense that I'm okay alone.

I don't have that deep terror, as I used to, of being left alone.

You have to "read' people really well to survive. That's part of being in an alcoholic family. You've got to know—Is he mad? Is he happy? What's the temperature today? What's going to tick him off? Part of good acting is responding to what you're getting. So I'm really good at noticing what I'm getting.

The divorce really made it hard to be connected to everyone. I had to make special time to be with my mom, my dad, my sisters. There is a lot of pressure. You lose out on that consistent support.

I have a closer relationship with all the people on my dad's side. But I think that it's bittersweet because I also feel torn because I'm not closer to my mother's side. My mom has one brother left and I rarely see him, so it's just my mom. I've been as close as I can to both parents now. All of us kids get together for the holidays and invite all the parents (mom, stepdad, dad, and stepmom) to one place so we don't have to schedule three Christmases. My mother is married again, to a wonderful man that we ALL love a lot, and it's good to see her happy. I remember the good times more than the bad, and I want them to know that I know they did the best they could.

Richard's Advice for Stepparents

Take time to get to know the child slowly.

You can't force a relationship that isn't there. If you walk in and there's pressure to see each other every single day and pressure to get married next week, you'll squish any possibility. And don't ask the kid to call you "Dad"! I think that's totally inappropriate; they're not your children and relationships have to develop.

Ted, a guy my mom dated for awhile, did the right thing. He didn't come with a goal in mind or a preconceived notion about exactly how this was going to turn out. He just came in and he was friendly. He got that I was definitely in a hard place, but he was friendly, playful, and light; and he didn't take things personally. He was just dating my mom and enjoying all of our company.

Respect and nourish the existing relationships.

You need to ask yourself the questions—What am I coming into? What are the relationships? If you marry a person, part of your responsibility is to nurture their relationships. As for my stepmom, she should have thought, "This guy that I'm marrying has a son in high school that wants to get close to his dad. Because I love my new husband, I really need to help him make that happen." Be supportive.

It would have been great if my stepmom had had the understanding and maturity to see that I wanted to get close to my dad. That's what a kid wants. So facilitate that. Encourage closeness with the two of them and join in when you can. Give them time alone and be really okay with that and light about it. But it's a natural thing to feel jealous or put out. You're just going to have to call your best friend and say, "Oh, this is so hard." That's not something you're going to share with the stepkid.

Richard's Advice for Parents

Don't force your kids to take sides.

Stay an adult and resist engaging your kids in who's right and who's wrong. It's so inappropriate. You need to reassure the child that regardless of all the issues, problems, and hatred, "I'm really glad you went to your dad's.

Sounds like you had a really good time; tell me all about it." And then go to your room later and burst into tears because you hate the son of a bitch. You married him and you had the kids; don't make them feel guilty because of your predicament. It's just not their problem. They can't be responsible for all that. They want to love both parents.

I think my mom played into it even more and said, you know, "Wow, your dad forgot your birthday." I mean, I kind of understood that he forgot, but to have her say how horrible it is that he forgot and have it reaffirmed by everybody else how horrible it was that he forgot, I think I developed this horrible feeling about it. And now that I'm older, all of us kids realize that he doesn't remember anybody's birthday. It's not personal. Now it's a joke. I know he adores me.

Oh yeah, I'd also say…don't get a divorce. It's the worst thing that happened to me. It fractured my life, my family, and my sense of security.

Intervene quickly if one parent is being put down.

If parents, regardless of the situation, hear anyone—grandmother, stepparent, or anyone else—make a disparaging remark about their child's father or mother, they should interrupt that right away, whether it's true or not. Say, "Hey, that's Richard's dad. Let's not talk about him like that." That's huge. Then the kid knows that he is safe, that he has an ally. That kind of talk won't be okay in this house. Also try to reaffirm how much the other parent loves the child. I had an aunt who would ask, "How is your mom?" It made me feel that I was a whole kid; I didn't come from just one parent.

You be the adult.

Kids need to know that they are loved, that they're going to be okay and that everything will be fine. There's all that forcing kids to be older than they are. There's no way that a high school student can solve the finances of a forty-year-old person. I didn't know anything about paying a mortgage in ninth grade and there's no way that I could handle that pressure and try and get through algebra and my French class too. I just couldn't. I had this utter and complete crushing pressure.

A kid just wants to solve the problem, especially a boy (and oldest son). All I wanted to do was solve the problem for my mom. She's crying; she has no job. When your mom's falling apart, you just feel like, "Oh, how can I help my mom? It's my job to fix it." She's saying, "I'm losing all my money and the house isn't going to sell," and "This job isn't working out and the money isn't coming in, you know. Jeez, times are really hard."

My father talked a lot about how hard it was and how little money he had. He was telling me that so I would go back to Mom and tell her how hard things were so that she would know why he wasn't paying the appropriate amount of support. I didn't need to know that. It felt so frightening. All I could think was "I'm in high school, and my parents don't have any money. They don't know what's next, and they're struggling. Well, are we all going to die?"

Keep those relationships clean. It's just an inappropriate shift in a relationship. You have to be the parent. There's a counselor and there's a client. And the counselor can't become a client. And with a parent, you have to stay a parent. What is a kid going to do with that adult information?

Don't make the kid get rid of their pets.

Kids have to have their pets. They've got to have something that stays the same. Pets could be the one connection they have. Divorce usually means kids have to be moved around. That's a big deal. I had to leave my dog, which was such a big deal. The dog was really my best friend and saving grace. They split the dogs in the divorce. My dad got one and my mom got the other. The one my dad got was the hunting dog that I had spent my childhood with. That was my best friend. That was really hard. I would call and ask how he was doing.

And those poor hamsters! She told us they would live in the wild. Come on, I knew they would be killed. Same with our cat. The cat was gone. So I started high school a week late in a new city. I lost a dog, a cat, all my hamsters, my family, and my home. I was worried about making dinner and getting a job while trying to pay attention in my civics class. It was a nightmare.

Pay attention.

With both my parents, there was a real lack of involvement about what was going on with me, a total disconnect. Parents need to ask, "What's happening with you guys? Is there a play or party? Are you on the track team?" My parents didn't go to plays or track meets. They weren't aware that I didn't bring home any homework. I registered myself into school; I signed all my own school paperwork. When I would cut school, I would sign my notes. I would throw birthday parties for myself. They were all totally disconnected from what was happening in my life.

Work as a team for the sake of the child.

Seeing your parents being friendly in the same room together is so great. It's not that you want your parents to get back together; you just want everyone to talk, be okay with each other and get along. Especially stepmom with mom, and stepdad with dad. It makes kids feel safe.

The happiest moments for all us kids were when the four of them started to talk and negotiate how the holidays were going to go. Before that, it was too hard for three kids to figure out what to do for summer vacation, Easter, and other holidays. Setting our own itinerary was hell. If we weren't lobbying to be with Dad, we were automatically with Mom; and if we did lobby to be with Dad it was a huge offense and a lot of guilt when we returned. And you really couldn't say you had a good time.

Get involved as a team and communicate what's happening. If there is a track meet on Saturday, work out who's going and get over all the marriage stuff for the kids. Just knowing that my parents had negotiated a plan to see me in something would have been enough.

Richard's Advice for Stepchildren

Divorce isn't about you.

Kids need to know that divorce is about these two adults and their relationship, and it doesn't have anything to do with anything you've said, done, or will do.

Find a neutral adult to talk with.

In high school when my parents divorced, I had a complete meltdown. I talked with one teacher who made a huge difference and all she did was listen. I'll never forget her; I still remember exactly where she was, and when and where we talked. It was probably an hour's worth of time, and it made all the difference. I just remember crying. Later I had a friend ten years older with a bad family life, and so we were able to commiserate. That helped.

■■■■■■■■■■■■■■■■■■■■■■■■■■■■■■■■

Nicole

Nicole is twenty-nine years old. Her parents never married. Her mother married her stepfather when Nicole was five; they separated when Nicole was seventeen. She has two half-sisters: her father's daughter who is three weeks older than Nicole, and the daughter of her mother and stepfather, seven years younger. Nicole is director of an after-school program. She recently broke up with her boyfriend of over seven years.

Nicole's Story

I lived with my mom, grandmother, Aunt Carol, Aunt Lisa, and Aunt Joan in my grandmother's house until I moved to live with my mom and stepdad when I was five. My Aunt Carol had my cousins Justin and Janea later, and they would come and go. People moved in and out all the time. It was nice because my aunts and grandma always surrounded me.

I still think of my grandmother's home as my home because that is where my good memories are. I had people to laugh and play with, and just hang out with. It was one of those comfortable environments. I got in trouble from time to time, but it was family. It was safe. I wasn't taken anywhere I didn't want to be, or put with anybody I didn't want to be with. It was the familiarity of it. I knew my cousins would come over to play, or I would go over to play with them. I always had someone there who cared about me. There was a routine. Certain things happened every year, like that chocolate calendar at Christmas.

My grandma has always been around. She is just grandma. She gives you vitamins or helps you pick things from the garden. We would go places with her, clean her house for money. But my Aunt Joan was my refuge.

I was always with my Aunt Joan. She took care of me a lot. My mom had me when she was twenty-one and started working right away to support me. Most of my memories are of being with my aunt, doing stuff with her, being in that house. She would do my birthday parties for me, and I would spend a lot of time with her and her husband. I still connect all my early memories with my Aunt Joan because she's the one who taught me board games and played with me.

Stepdad

My real dad and mom were never married. I was five just turning six when my mom married my stepfather, who had children from a previous marriage. I remember him before they got married, and my mom says that even then I didn't like him. I don't think they had a wedding. I think they just went to the Justice of the Peace.

The next thing I knew, my mom and I moved from the house where we had lived for five years with her sisters and mom to a whole new place. I don't remember my mom telling me that we were going to move in with my stepdad; I just remember being in a new house in a different part of town. That was it.

I remember I didn't like my stepdad. I just didn't like him from the time I was two. My mom tells me that one time I was sitting between the two of them on the couch, and I leaned over to bite his hand. I remember one time when I reached into his plate, he slapped my hand. I wasn't used to punishment. My aunts would talk to me and explain things to me. At that moment I really didn't like him.

There was one time after we moved into the new house I got in trouble, and I remember the spanking I got from that. After that I knew I never wanted to set him off where he had to lay a hand on me again. I was afraid of him. He was a big guy and pretty intimidating. I tried to do what I was supposed to do around the house, so I wouldn't get into trouble.

My mom told me she never made me call him Dad, but one of her friends who babysat for me said I had to call him Dad, and he agreed. That's when it seemed like a reality to me. "Wow. I'm living here with him and her, and I don't like him." Before that, he was kind of like another person to me. I didn't think about it much, but after the move I thought, "I've moved to a new place and I'm not around my aunts and my family anymore."

I mostly stayed in my room. I'd get up Saturday morning at 6:00 on the dot, eat my cereal, and watch cartoons all day. I felt alone so I just built my own little wall. I remember that there were things in the house I couldn't touch even though I lived there. I never was in their room hanging out with them. I always knocked on the door. I always felt separate. I really missed my aunt. I would go back to my Aunt Joan's or my grandmother's and that's where I would get my familiar things. That was my family. The next year I remember my mom being pregnant and them arguing.

Middle school was when things got really bad. I don't think I even wanted to have a relationship with him by the time I got to that age. He was mean to me. Then I was a senior in high school and that was it for me. I knew what was going on.

I remember them fighting a lot. One particular time I remember them yelling and then the sound of him hitting her. I told him to stop hitting my mom. He told me to get out of there. And I just remember the look on my mother's face. She didn't know what to do. So I ran upstairs and called my grandmother, who lived next door. My little sister was trying to get downstairs and kept yelling, "Daddy, daddy." I told her she couldn't go down there. Much later he tried to apologize. I thought, "Whatever." There was nothing he could have said to make it better. I just knew he had hit my mom. I heard it, and I knew it. That was it.

The next year my mom, my sister and I moved out. They separated, but their divorce was not finalized until later. And then at some point he needed a place to live and came to live with us again for a month or so. I was so angry.

I have a few happy memories of him. We always took family trips to the mountains, and there was one time when I was in fourth grade when he helped me learn how to long jump. That made me happy. Other than that, I don't have any memories that show I bonded with him or wanted to sit on his lap or talk to him. I kind of felt, "You are just somebody who is living here."

Real Dad, "just James"

Even today I don't have any relationship with my real father. It's really shaky. He's trying, but I haven't accepted him. I remember him taking me to Betty Boop movies. And I remember spending the night at his house with my sister Bridget when I was about four. Bridget is my half-sister. My dad was married to her mom when he met my mom. He didn't tell my mom he was married.

My dad spent more time in my half-sister's life because he was married to her mother. When I was in the seventh grade, a mutual friend reunited my sister and me. That's when he re-entered the picture. He would take us shopping. Sometimes I thought he was just showing me off to his friends, and I felt used. I liked his sisters and my cousins, but I don't keep in touch with them.

I shut myself off from him getting to know me. I loved my half-sister, and we built a relationship, but I closed myself off to him. I still see him every now and then, but it's still really hard. We fight and fight, and I just can't listen to him. I feel that all he does is lie. I feel that he should respect me more. When I go back home, I don't tell him. It's hard on my sister. She has a relationship with him and can't understand why I don't. He's just James to me, not my father. He wants to be a part of my life, but I know I'm going to keep him at a distance. There are things we need to talk about.

Mom and Sisters

My relationship with my mom has always been good. Could I imagine going through what she's gone through? She was always trying to survive. I was happier after my stepfather left when it was just me, my mom, and my sister living in the house together. She would always make my dresses for dances and different occasions. She always took us to plays. We did a lot more together. In my senior year in high school, I was unhappy because she had made the decision to let him come back. She knew I didn't like him. She knew how I felt from the time I was two. I'd like to ask my mother why she decided to marry a person I didn't like. If she knew I didn't like him at two, why did she marry him? It should have mattered to her. It would have mattered to me.

Now our relationship is better. I confide in her as I do in my Aunt Joan. She knows me now and accepts me and knows what I will and will not deal with. We've worked at it. She tried to do the best she could. I love her. I can imagine how hard it was for her trying to make it with two daughters. She tried to do it the best way possible. I see her strength. She has made me strong. She has never re-married. Today she has a new boyfriend, and he's all right. I just want my mother to have the best.

I have good relationships with my stepsiblings. Bridget is three and one-half weeks older than me. I call her for advice. I love her. I like her mom. She's accepted me. I just feel how sad it was for her and my mom to go through what they went through. When my half-sister Kim came, I tried to take care of her because then I had someone to look after. I would sit downstairs and hold her and watch *Sesame Street*. We each claimed our mom as our own. She was just struggling as I was. Her dad (my stepdad) kind of disappeared. She's struggling with that.

Lasting Effects

I believe the stepchild experience has affected my life today. I'm attracted to older men. I look for some kind of knowledge, something from them to guide me. I try to figure men out, but they really haven't been a stable part of my life. I have to say it's really been hard. All my relationships have been long-term. Maybe that's because I hold on to them. Maybe it's the same thing my mom did.

I can relate to kids really well. There was this little girl I worked with. Her real problem was at home. Her parents had separated, her mom had a new boyfriend, and she felt her mom ignored her. She had somebody living in her house she didn't know anything about. That's hard— I know.

I have a family. They've taken care of me and have been there for me through the ups and downs. I've learned that a family doesn't need to have a man in it, but I would have liked a positive male in my life, another strong presence. I've always wanted to have a "complete" family like my best friend. She has a dad who talks with her about things. She can go to him for information about men in her life. I see it as a balance; she has two sides to go to. That's a complete family. I have all these women in my life. It's been like one side of the story.

Nicole's Advice for Stepparents

Let the child know you care.

Talk with the child and let him or her know who you are and what you're about. It would have benefited my stepfather to tell me— "This is where I come from, these are my kids, and this is why I love them, and this is why I want to be a part of your life and love you." It would have made a difference for me to know that they were not separate from me, they could be a part of everything I experienced, they could be my brothers and sisters too, and he could be my dad. I felt so separate.

There was no explanation from him. It was like, "I'm in the house and I'm going to be your stepfather. And that's it." There wasn't anything friendly about it. If he had opened up and said, "I love your mom, and I want to get to know you and hopefully you'll let me do that. And maybe I can help you with different things at different times." Maybe I would have accepted him and maybe not, but I would have had that memory of him.

Make an effort to find out about the child.

Don't think that things are going to be automatically great. See what the kid likes, not because you'll get in good with them, but because you genuinely have an interest and want to find a connection with that child. If my stepdad had come to my games and events, it would have mattered. It would have created a bond. We could have talked about sports or something.

And if the kid hates you, make an effort to understand why. You can't let it go and not ask why. You need to really talk with your stepchild. Maybe the kid is close to the rest of the family, like the aunts and uncles. Talk with them about it. That would have helped. My Aunt Joan could have said, "You know she loves playing *Sorry* and she loves playing *Speed*. She loves listening to music with me. Do those things with her."

Nicole's Advice for Parents

Prepare the child to move to the new house.

It was a big move for me. I left the home where I grew up. Kids remember those things. Take the kid to the new place. Explain—"Here's the new house. You're going to have your own room. We're going to decorate it. Your aunts can still come over. We're going to do some things to work it out. Your aunts will come over and take you out."

Create time for the child to get to know the step-parent.

Maybe my mom could have done more to help me accept him. I don't think I would just get married to someone and tell my kids, "Oh, this is your stepdad, and he's going to be moving in with you in a week. I know you've been living here for a while, but we're moving to a new house, and we might not be next to your aunts anymore. We might not see them that often." I could never imagine myself doing that. Working with kids, I see how their feelings are and how easily things affect them. You have to know as an adult that something like that would affect them some way or another.

And if it means not getting married right away, then it means not getting married right away. It means that you're going to wait until a relationship with this person and your child is established. You want some kind of stable foundation, so there won't be a rift between the two of them. If this isn't done, things can only get worse as far as I'm concerned. And it's harder on an older kid. I was just a little kid. If the child is young, it's easier to find activities to do together. This will gradually get the child ready for the move or transition, and it has to happen up front before the decision to get married.

If things are not going well with the stepparents, do something about it.

If you see that your kid doesn't like the stepparent, and they're keeping their distance, you need to do something. If I saw problems, I would take the initiative to work things out. It would hurt me if things weren't clicking in my household. I would talk to my kid and ask, "What's going on? I notice that you're really having a hard time with your stepdad. Is there anything you need to know about him that I haven't told you about? Do you have any questions?" I would make the kid feel safe coming to me if he or she had problems.

Nicole's Advice for Stepchildren

Keep busy.

I like to be out doing things, being active. My mom supported that. It helps take your mind off of things. It gives you a release. It helps you get out that extra energy that maybe you can't release at home.

In middle school, I would go to track events and run. In high school, I got involved in student council, pep club, basketball, track, and marching band. By the time I had graduated, I had narrowed it to track, student council, and cheerleading. The activities kept me out during the week. I was happy with that. I had practice, and then I would come home, study, and go to bed. I loved it.

Find good friends.

I have one really close friend I've known since I was four. She's my only friend that has her mom and dad together. Her family is my family. Her mother asks, "How's my other daughter doing?" I call her mother "Mom," and she's always checking on me. I have met all her extended family. They even invited me to her dad's parents' sixtieth wedding anniversary.

The only stable male I have had is my best friend's dad. Her dad cares about me. I know I could go to him and he would tell it to me straight. He has a lot of brothers and they're like my uncles. They just love me.

Try to find an adult to talk to.

Sometimes you don't feel comfortable talking with your parents. You need a neutral person in your life, someone you can talk to. I felt really safe going to Aunt Joan. She was always caring, supportive, and clear. She would ask questions. I would tell her everything. She was the person I told when I had my first intimate relationship. I remember doing everything with her, from losing my teeth to playing on the playground to planning birthday parities. Joan was always there. Her kids were like my own sisters. We had one fight in our lives. It was heartbreaking. That will never happen again.

■ ■

Reflections

When I think of family, the image that flashes before my eyes is a black-and-white, 8x10, grainy photograph of my father, two older brothers, and the rest of the "Hoot Owls" posing for their annual team picture. That photograph, which has been a fixture in my parents' guest room for the past forty-five years, tells the story of my childhood. Each Sunday morning during baseball season, my dad, mom, three brothers, and I would make our weekly trek to the neighborhood ballpark for the "big game." We each had our role. My father coached, my brother David pitched, my brother Mike played first base, my mom, with my baby brother Rob playing in his baby carriage beside her, worked the concession stand, and I became the "bat person," handing out the perfect bat to each hitter. Girls were not allowed to play Little League baseball in the 50's. Even today, that photo brings back the pungent smells of tar and freshly mowed grass; the taste of Abba Zabbas, cotton candy, and licorice; and the excitement I felt in the pit of my stomach on Sunday mornings before the start of each game.

Family for my husband Art was six o'clock dinner. He remembers how his father would come out of the house minutes before six and, in a whistle that could be heard for miles, beckon Art to leave his daily pick-up game at the neighborhood park and run home for dinner. Then as a family they would gather around the kitchen table of their modest working-class home in Inglewood to eat dinner and share their day, a ritual that was repeated every day, rain or shine, except during football season when Art would arrive a few minutes late from practice.

While six o'clock dinners and Sunday baseball games defined our 1950's concept of family, for the stepchildren speaking here, duffle bags, airplane tickets, and freeways serve as more appropriate symbols of their family experience. Always on the move, with their trusted duffle bag by their side, stepchildren travel back and forth from family to family, constantly adjusting to different people, houses, rules, schedules, and even value systems. The same was true in the stepfamily Art and I created when our marriage brought together our four children from previous relationships. I can still remember those Sunday nights when we would "exchange" the children. With my husband impatiently honking his horn, my stepkids would whip around the house, stuffing everything they could find into their duffle bags—jeans, shirts, underwear, school books, homework, and when they were younger, their favorite stuffed animal—as they prepared to go to their mom's house. It was utter chaos, and it took its toll. Recently when I asked my stepson David if he ever planned to move from the "dream house" he shares with his wife and two baby daughters, he shook his head slowly and said, "We'll never move." And then after a moment he added, "We're keeping it in trust for my children who will live there forever after we're gone." I believe him.

For better or worse, by the year 2010, most kids in this country will be schlepping their duffle bags back and forth from family to family. For better or worse, with divorce on the rise, stepfamilies are here to stay. The question becomes: How can we make them work? We know from the statistics that like those in this book, most stepfamilies struggle. We know from the stepchildren who speak here that building stepfamilies can be painful. But the stepchildren also want us to know that as hard as it was for them, it doesn't have to be that way for you. By reading their stories and looking at their advice you can learn how to do this better. And that of course is why the stepchildren agreed to tell their stories in the first place.

What did they teach us about how we can "do this better"?

To parents:

I begin with what I consider to be the most important observation: The success or failure of the stepfamily rests with the parents. The stepchildren tell us that it is parents, not stepparents or children, that make or break the new family. What does this mean? For starters, it means that the parents are responsible for clarifying everyone's role in the new family. Who sets the rules? Who disciplines the children? Who talks with the other parent? And who takes the children to the doctor, dentist, back-to-school night, and baseball and ballet practice? The day-to-day stuff of every family. This is especially important in the early stages of a stepfamily when everyone is walking on thin ice, trying to get along, sorting out the new relationships. Once the new family is set up, it is the responsibility of the parents to check in regularly to make sure that things are not "slipping through the cracks." Our stepchildren recommend that parents schedule regular family meetings (Sophia calls them "reuniones de familia") to discuss how things are going, what's working and what isn't. The stepchildren tell us that open and honest communication is one of the keys to a successful stepfamily.

Parents must teach the stepparent about their new children. In stepfamilies, adults and children come into each other's lives as total strangers. They share no history, no traditions, and no memories. They are like blank slates to each other. Perhaps that explains the awkwardness many stepchildren feel around their new stepparent, especially at the beginning. Imagine living with someone you may not know, sharing the bathroom, discussing your day over breakfast, and planning your next vacation. These are the kinds of things we do with people we know and trust, not with strangers. As Sophia says, "When there is a new member in the family, one is acutely aware of self."

Parents can do many things to help. Show your spouse old photos of your children at different stages of their lives, share their achievements, take out the basketball and spelling bee trophies, tell them funny anecdotes, and let them know what foods your children like and don't like—anything and everything that can help "fill in the blanks." On a related note, the stepchildren also tell us that they would like to learn about their stepparents as well, especially before they move in together. They would like to spend time alone with their stepparents, learn about their job, their history, and their hobbies. They may discover they have interests in common. Who knows? It could happen.

Last, the stepchildren feel strongly that when there are problems in the new family, whether big or small, parents need to take action immediately. Don't let things slide. Don't be passive. As Sebastian reminds us, it is not unusual for stepparents to have issues with their stepchildren, and for stepchildren to have issues with their stepparents. He urges parents to pay attention. "Are there signs of aggression? Are the stepchildren being picked on too much? Are they having too many chores to do? Are they being spanked too much? Is there a lot of hollering going on? Remember that children cannot defend themselves. Talk with the stepparent. Take action." Nicole recommends that parents shouldn't even think about getting married until their children and new spouse have established a loving and healthy relationship. "You want some kind of stable foundation so there won't be a rift between the two of them," says Nicole. "If this isn't done, things can only get worse as far as I'm concerned."

The stepchildren also remind us how important it is for parents to intervene when they hear anyone putting down the other parent. Maya describes how it feels when this doesn't happen. "When you're a kid, you're in a fantasy world. Then there's this person coming into your fantasy world saying bad things about your parents. You don't tell that to a child. I'm sorry. That stuff is just too adult. It's just not nice. Because what can the child do? She's not in a position that she can do anything. If you're only five years old, you can't go and get your own job and say, 'I'm out of here. I don't need to hear this.' So it makes you schizophrenic internally." Richard takes this one step further by advising parents and other family members to confront this head-on. "'Hey, that's Richard's dad. Let's not talk about him like that. That kind of talk won't be okay in this house.' Then the kid knows that he is safe, that he has an ally."

The stepchildren also have advice for parents who do not live with their children on a full-time basis, the so-called "weekend parents." For children, family is about the details and stories of daily life. It is about the tragic untimely death of a goldfish, the challenging physics teacher, the nervousness of a first date, and the excitement about graduation. These are the things families talk about over dinner, the events that become family legend. When parents do not live with their children, they often miss out on these details and stories. The goal for these parents is to figure out how to make up for that loss. The stepchildren recommend that parents find a way to communicate often and consistently with their kids, and as Maya reminds us, "Make the contact real." Sam suggests that you write things down as you speak so that when you call the next time, you will remember to ask about them. He reminds us, "When you live with someone you don't have to do that because you know what's going on each day. But when you don't, there could have been a major event that had its beginning, middle, and end already, and it's passed and you don't know about it."

This can only happen when the parents are on speaking terms, and as we know from the stepchildren in this book, communication between parents is often fraught with tension and hostility, especially in the first few years following a divorce. But the stepchildren make it clear that they want their parents to put aside their anger and resentment so they can work together as a team for the sake of their kids. As Richard tells us, "It's not that you want your parents to get back together, you just want everyone to talk, be okay with each other and get along. Especially stepmom with mom, and stepdad with dad. It makes kids feel safe." Sam adds. "It sends a message to the children that they're important, important enough to both parents that when it comes to their children's needs, they can work things out, even if it's as simple as sending a check."

To stepparents:

Your stepchildren do not want to hate you. Contrary to popular lore, stepchildren want to like you and to be liked by you. As Julie says, they may put up a bit of fuss at the beginning, but you can easily win them over. In their heart of hearts, they want you to be another caring adult in their lives. They want you to attend their ballet recitals, basketball games, and back-to-school night, hold their hand when they go to the doctor, and comfort them when they come home with a "D" in chemistry. They want you to be "parent-like."

But the stepchildren also tell us that we should never, ever try and take the place of their "real" mom or dad. This will not work. Don't take this personally. It is not about you. Try not to get into the "what am I, chopped liver?" syndrome, when after you've driven your stepchild all over town and back, all they really want to do is rush home so they can share the details with their "real" dad or mom. Stop, take a deep breath, and try to remember that while your stepchildren want you in their lives, they have a mom and they have a dad. As Sam says, "If you are a stepfather, recognize that there is another father. If you're the stepmother, recognize that there is a mother. You can't be that person and should not try to be a substitute for that person. Your relationship should be important on its own terms." Sophia says of her stepfather, "He went slowly so that I never felt threatened or that he was forcing his way into my life as a father. He was a friend first; once I felt comfortable with him, be became a father figure."

How do you develop a good relationship with your stepchildren on "your own terms"? The stepchildren advise us to take the relationship slowly and allow it to develop naturally. Show by words and deeds that you genuinely care about them. Ask questions. Find common interests. Stock your refrigerator with their favorite foods. And, perhaps most important, arrange to do things together. Take hikes, go to the movies, play chess, create art, go to baseball games, and go shopping for clothes. But as Kate reminds us, start slowly. "Don't just go on a weekend together. That's a lot of togetherness. How about a little dinner?"

To children:

The stepchildren have three important things to say to other stepchildren. First, do not blame yourself for your parents' problems. You did not cause them and you cannot fix them. Stay a child. As Kate says, "You can never be fifteen again." The stepchildren also encourage other stepchildren to find a way to express their feelings. As

Sebastian says, "If something's bothering you and you're feeling kind of sad and hurting and it's in your heart, you should really talk about it. Make it known. Tell somebody. Opening up and confiding in somebody is the most important thing. Don't keep secrets."

The final thing they want stepchildren to know is that there are adults in the world who can help. Children do not have to face their problems alone. Nicole turned to her Aunt Joan, Richard to his teacher, Maya to the family of her friend, and Sebastian to Sister Lillian. Most turned to grandparents, especially grandmothers, for the refuge they so desperately needed.

Grandparents are often the one constant in children's lives. They represent stability and continuity. When all else changes, they don't; when all others leave, they don't. Sophia's grandparents moved from Puerto Rico to Los Angeles to be help raise her and her brothers. Her grandfather took on the role of father when her biological father "did not step up to the role." Indeed when her grandfather's life was ending, he told her," I do not want to die. Who will take care of your mom, you, and your brothers"? As Sam says about his grandmother, "I visited her house a lot as I was growing up. She always understood people. There was not a problem between two people that she couldn't figure out something to say to make it better. She could break it down. There wasn't much that I wouldn't talk with her about."

The most important decision I made after my divorce from my son's dad was to make sure that my son consistently spent time with both sets of grandparents. I have wonderful memories of my parents telling him stories about growing up in the immigrant neighborhoods of New York, the same stories they told my brothers and me as we were growing up. My father would describe hot summer nights in the Bronx playing stickball on the streets with hundreds of neighborhood kids whose parents gave them names like "Free Thought" and "Free Love." They would laugh and laugh as my dad in his thickest Yiddish accent would yell, "Free Thought Ginsburg, come home for dinner." My mom would talk about the continuous stream of cousins, aunts, and uncles that would stay with her after they got off the boat from Russia, and how her dad, my grandfather, would help them find jobs and housing. These stories helped my son understand that he belonged to a large family with deep roots and old traditions. Richard says almost the same thing, "All those long conversations with my grandmother finally paid off in New York where I would remember a strong, working-class, farming family. I could tell myself, 'I'm from good people. I'm a good person.'"

This need to belong, to be part of a larger family is a theme that weaves throughout all the stories, and the stepchildren have taught us that when an intact family falls apart, people can build new families from the materials they have at hand. Some like Nicole and Maya found that sense of belonging with the family of their friends. "Her family became my family," says Nicole. "I call her mother, Mom." Adds Maya, "The family of one of my friends took me on their vacations with them. They were my family."

Others have created their own version of family, a blend of the old and the new. For them, family is much more inclusive than the "blood is thicker than water" version in which Art and I were raised. For us, family meant parents, siblings, grandparents, aunts, uncles and cousins. It rarely included friends. For the stepchildren, family includes but is not limited to blood relationships. As Sophia says, "It goes beyond blood to people I trust. I see myself raising my child in this network of people who will be aunts and uncles." Adds Errol, "I learned that family is the people you hold close to your heart and not necessarily the people you popped out of. Family is the people you take to and make as your family."

Whether they joined other families or established new ones, the stepchildren have taught us that at their core, all families have the same goal. Sam speaks for all the stepchildren when he says, "When I think about what a family should do, it's to facilitate the betterment of everyone who's in them." Who could possibly disagree with that?

■■■■■■■■■■■■■■■■■■■■■■■■■■■■■■■■■

Epilogue

My son is now 34, and my stepchildren are 32, 30 and 27. Three are married and one is in a committed relationship. The four children call themselves a family and call each other brother and sister. I have planned dozens of birthday parties, weddings, and baby showers with Ruth, the mother of my stepchildren. And when my stepson and his wife had their first child, they named her after her two great-grandmothers, one of which was my mother. We are a success story, a model of what a stepfamily can be at its best. I don't want to mislead you; we didn't get there quickly and we didn't get there easily. But we got there.

■■■■■■■■■■■■■■■■■■■■■■■■■■■■■■■■■■

About the Author

Susan Philips is a Senior Consultant for the Constitutional Rights Foundation (CRF), a national citizenship and law-related educational organization. She also consults with LACER Hollywood Stars, an organization that promotes arts and literacy in middle schools in Los Angeles. Susan received a Master's degree in Journalism from the University of Southern California. This is her first book. Susan lives in Los Angeles.

Would you like additional copies of *Stepchildren Speak*?

Order from: **AYWN Publications**
                1209 Officers' Row
                Vancouver, WA 98661

We accept checks and purchase orders. If you would like to use a credit card, please go to our website **www.aywnpublications.com** to use PayPal. Questions? Call 360-695-1010.

Please deliver my book(s) to:

Name_____

Address _____

City_____State ____ Zip _____

Phone _____

Each *Stepchildren Speak* is $14.95 plus $2.50 shipping ($4 Priority mail). Quantities of 2 or more receive a 10% discount. Add 7% of the total price to cover shipping of orders of more than one copy.

Quantity	Individual Price	Total Price
10% discount for quantities over 1		
Shipping		
Total Cost		

Check our web site to find other publications
for parents and teachers
www.aywnpublications.com